To Charlene,

    May God continue to guide and bless all your journeys in life and fill your heart with joy and peace.

Kenneth Widdess
The Peacewalker

We are called to journey in this life: To walk in peace, Like a

gentle river flowing through a lush green valley, To walk in love,

Like the golden  sun radiating its

light and warmth upon our needy

earth, To walk in God's presence,

Like the deer that thirsts after

the high mountain brooks and is completely satisfied.

Many of our journeys will be long, yet what we learn along the

way will instill faith, hope and the courage to live in peace.

The Appalachian Trail follows the Franconia Ridge over Mt. Lincoln and Little Haystack Mountain

Hiking near the summit of Glastenbury Mountain (3,748 feet) in the Green Mountain National Forest, VT.

Sojourn In The Wilderness

A Seven Month Journey On The Appalachian Trail

Kenneth Wadness

Foreword by Bill Irwin, author of Blind Courage

HARMONY HOUSE
PUBLISHERS LOUISVILLE

Dedication

This book is dedicated to all people who

desire to be peacewalkers, whether they sojourn in the cities or

the country, in their neighborhoods, or in foreign

lands, along the ocean or in the mountains.

Executive Editors: William Strode
Library of Congress Catalog Number 97-071299
Hardcover International Standard Book Number 1-56469-034-2
Printed in Hong Kong
First Edition printed Summer 1997 by Harmony House Publishers,
P.O. Box 90, Prospect, Kentucky 40059 (502) 228-2010 / 228-4446
Copyright © 1997 by Ken Wadness
Photographs copyright © 1997 by Ken Wadness
Cover Design & Production Assistance: Robert L. Williams, Jr.

*Title Page Photograph: The Appalachian Trail near Cold River, VT. The Appalachian and the Long Trail
follow one another for about 100 miles from Mt. Killington to the Massachusetts border.*

*Cover Photograph: Appalachian Trail on Silver Hill near the Hoosatonic River,
Cornwall Bridge, CT.*

Acknowledgement

No one can complete a significant journey without loving help from family and friends. It is with deep appreciation and gratitude – and a sincere desire that they experience God's greatest blessings – that I mention those who assisted me in my "Sojourn in the Wilderness."

Thanks, Mom and Dad, for all your love and support during this journey. Your efforts in buying extra items, keeping everything organized and sending me all my mail drops were invaluable.

Thanks, Gary, for being such a wonderful brother and for meeting me at Mt. Katahdin, taking me home from Bear Mountain in New York and picking me up from Georgia at the end of the journey.

Thanks, Sondra, for your love and all the hard work you put into each aspect of this experience: food preparations and mail drops as well as being with me at the start of the journey in Maine and meeting me at various places along the way. Also, no words can express the depth of my gratitude for your tireless labors over this text from start to finish.

Thanks, Steve (The Great White Bowana), for giving me the encouragement and wisdom I needed before I began the journey.

Thanks to Steve and Lisa, Jay Fred and Peggy, Jeff and Suzie, Bill and Mae, and Ronnie and Julie for allowing me to stay in your homes and meeting so many of my needs.

Thanks, Paul and Mary, for picking me up at the end of my journey and letting me live in your peaceful home for more than three weeks. Thanks to Jerry and Sophie and Leo and Bobbie for allowing me to use your homes as havens for the writing of this book.

Thanks to Yitzie, Wayne, Cheryl, Karen, Bettye and Eddie for all the advice and time you took in looking over various drafts of the manuscript.

Thanks, Larry, for being such a great editor and for putting your time and effort into this project.

Thanks to Debbie, Justin, Sara and Katlin for your help in preparing the book materials to be sent to the publishers.

Most of all, I thank God for the opportunity and privilege of hiking the Appalachian Trail and seeing the journey go to this stage of completion and beyond – to more of life's awesome opportunities.

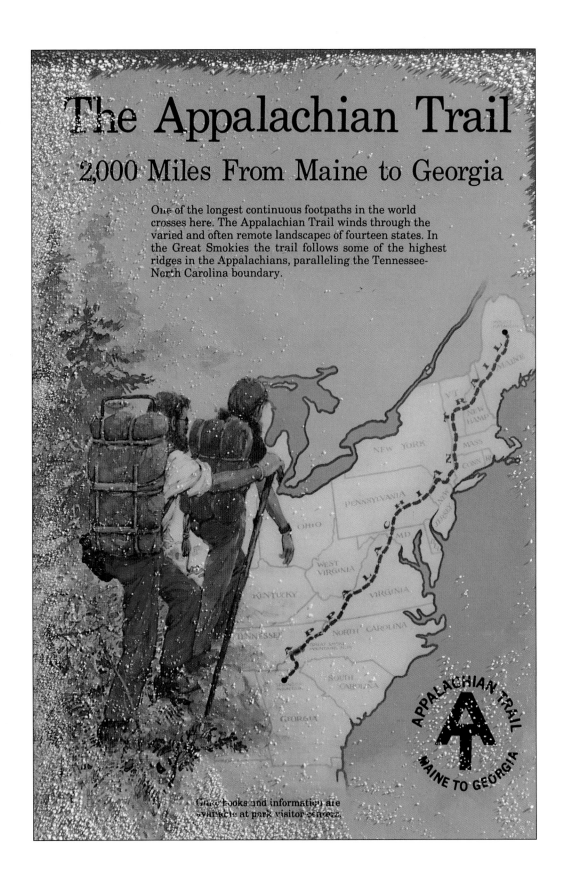

The Appalachian Trail

2,000 Miles From Maine to Georgia

One of the longest continuous footpaths in the world crosses here. The Appalachian Trail winds through the varied and often remote landscapes of fourteen states. In the Great Smokies the trail follows some of the highest ridges in the Appalachians, paralleling the Tennessee-North Carolina boundary.

Guide books and information are available at park visitor centers.

Preface

One cold autumn day I was traveling with a friend on the Massachusetts Turnpike. It was nearly dusk, and we were passing through the Berkshire Mountains when I looked up at a bridge crossing the highway and noticed a sign that read "**Appalachian Trail.**" Soon, as if in a dream, I saw myself as a hiker standing on the bridge while walking that famous footpath. Although I had often passed under that highway sign on other occasions, it seemed that I had never really seen it until that moment. I knew little about the trail, but I pictured myself wandering over rugged mountains and through pristine valleys. In this way, almost instantaneously, a desire to hike the entire trail was born in my heart.

More than a decade passed before I took my first step on the long, arduous journey described in this book. As each year passed, I thought often about this great wilderness adventure, asking myself, "Could this possibly be the year that God opens the door for this journey?" I loved the outdoors and had learned camping skills at a summer camp I attended as a child and which I later served as a counselor. Yet most of my hiking experience consisted of day hikes and a few weekend outings in the White Mountains of New Hampshire. There was much I needed to learn. So I read books on the trail and asked questions of anyone who knew anything about it. Over the years my knowledge of the trail and understanding of wilderness survival progressed even though I hiked only occasionally.

The Appalachian Trail materialized from the efforts of a man named Benton MacKaye in the early 1900s. MacKaye dreamed of forming a wilderness refuge where urban workers could find refreshment after toiling in factories. In 1925 the Appalachian Trail Conference was formed to coordinate the work of hundreds of trail-building volunteers, and in August of 1937 a Civilian Conservation Corps crew opened the last section of trail on a high ridge connecting Spalding and Sugarloaf Mountains in Maine. The Appalachian Trail was 2,025 miles long then. Later, due to encroaching civilization and the effects of the weather, it needed to be relocated in many places. In 1968 Congress established the walkway as the first National Scenic Trail, giving the National Park Service authority to acquire the land needed to maintain trail continuity. Today less than 40 of the 2,160 miles of the Appalachian Trail remain on private land. A magnificent resource created by many dedicated people, the trail is now maintained by thousands of other volunteers who love the outdoors and want to see the trail preserved.

The mystique of hiking the entire trail began to develop in 1948 when a man from Pennsylvania, Earl Shaffer, became the first person to "thru-hike" from Georgia to Maine. A thru-hiker is a person who tries to hike the trail in one continuous effort. Walking the trail from end to end, or in sections, has grown in popularity over the years. By 1969 only 50 people had hiked the full trail, but by 1975 there were 300. Today more than 3,000 people, young and old, have done this.

My long wait to hike the trail served a great purpose – for my spiritual life, which became important to me during these years, was an integral part of my journey. On this trek along the crest of the Appalachian Mountains, my faith in God was tried more times than I can recount. Also, I am an avid nature photographer, and as I matured spiritually, I became more creative in my photographic technique, and it seemed that my perception of the beauty of the natural world was being enhanced.

More than 95 percent of thru-hikers start in Georgia and end in Maine, thus avoiding the mosquitoes and black flies of the New England spring, the wintry weather of the southern Appalachians and the loneliness inherent in a southbound trek. As an elementary school teacher, with work responsibilities that come to an end temporarily in June each year, I found it impossible to start my hike in Georgia. I had to become one of the few who hike south, beginning in Maine. Over the years, while talking with friends about my dream of hiking the trail, I noticed that no one volunteered to go with me. Perhaps I knew from the beginning that I would make the trip alone, and I certainly knew that the odds of my completing the journey were against me. Still, as winter gripped New England in 1990, I decided not to return to the teaching position I had held for the previous five years. I was resolved to embark on an adventure that would change my life.

In preparing for this I was fortunate to meet a man named Steve, who had hiked most of the trail in 1981. He helped me plan for meals, the most difficult aspect of organizing a long-distance hike. To make dinners more appetizing, Steve suggested that I have a ten-day rotation of evening meals. Most of these would consist of rice, noodles, Sloppy Joe mix, soups and macaroni and cheese. (See appendix on "Food" for more details.) In the spring I bought most of the food for the hike in bulk quantities. I also borrowed Steve's large dehydrator and dried more than 80 pounds of vegetables, spaghetti sauce, hamburger, and Sloppy Joe dinners.

Through the Appalachian Trail Conference, located in Harpers Ferry, W.Va., I obtained indispensable trail guides and maps. These not only provided distances on segments of the trail, but told of water, shelter and camping locations as well as road crossings and parking spots. I also received a list of "trail towns," communities either on the trail or not far from it where hikers can replenish supplies, wash clothes, shower, and eat as much good food as possible. Post offices in most of these towns will hold packages and letters for up to a month or two until designated thru-hikers come to pick them up. I chose 18 trail towns, the distances from one to another ranging from 70 to more than 150 miles. So when I began, 18 pre-addressed and numbered boxes were stacked on the floor of my room at home. When I called home from a trail town, I would ask my father to mail the next one or two so they would arrive well ahead of me. Each box contained the food I needed to get to the next town, along with extra clothes or supplies. In some towns I purchased basic food items like peanut butter, jelly, cheese, and bread or bagels. Many towns had various accommodations for thru-hikers. I stayed in a few bed-and-breakfasts, inns, barns, and motels, but mostly in church-sponsored hostels. One night I slept alongside four beautiful red trucks in a fire station.

In reading about the trail, I learned that most hikers do not go by their real names but by trail names. Some receive trail names from other hikers, most, however, choose their own. For many it can be difficult to decide on a trail name. This was true of me. However, one day in the late spring as I was driving home from school, an idea popped into my mind. My Hebrew name, Shalom, which was given to me at birth, means peace. So I chose "Peacewalker," a name that expressed my heart's desire to walk in peace with God in the wilderness. I wanted this "Sojourn in the Wilderness" to change my life in such a way that I would come to be a blessing to people I met on the trail and in the years to come.

So this book is more than just an account of my hike. It records a spiritual journey as well. My intention for you, the reader, is that you not only walk with me in the Appalachian wilderness and experience the peace and beauty of God's creation, but also sense the struggles of living daily in the mountains. Because my faith in God is based on the Bible, I have endeavored to share thoughts that came to my mind and heart from God as I wandered down the trail. I hope the insights I had will encourage you in your life's journey by strengthening your faith and helping you find, as I have, a greater sense of peace.

As July drew near, my preparations were nearly complete. I recall clearly the ordeal of trying to put into my pack what I thought I needed for the first hundred miles. Over the years I had purchased a lot of equipment – too much, of course. Every hiker I talked to had told me to take only items I would use each day. "If you don't use it every day, you don't need it," they said. With all my stuff laid out on my living room floor, I tried to load my large external-frame backpack. It took me hours to figure out what was essential and what was not. This experience, a nightmare, was already testing my strength and faith. A northbound thru-hiker I eventually met on the trail told me that when he was beginning his journey at Amicalola Falls State Park, about eight miles south of

Springer Mountain in Georgia, he watched with interest as a potential thru-hiker, having been driven to the park by friends, struggled to fit into his pack all the things he had brought. After an hour of frustration and anger, he threw his pack and gear into the trunk of his friend's car, and they drove off. He never took a step on the trail.

With everything in it I thought I needed, I tried to lift my pack off the floor. It was so heavy that I had to sit on the floor, put myself in the arm straps, roll onto my knees and then push myself up. After weighing myself with the pack on, I subtract-ed my weight and discovered that the pack was 80 pounds – an amount I had never carried. As I stood there disconsolately, leaning awkwardly forward to keep myself balanced, I looked into my father's tear-filled eyes, and I too began to cry, not knowing what lay ahead. My friend Sondra, who had packaged food, labeled boxes, and provided encouragement for weeks, helped me get the huge pack into the trunk of her car. We then headed north for Maine, bound for Baxter State Park, and within it Mt. Katahdin, the northern end of the famed Appalachian Trail.

The summit of Mt. Katahdin, ME. Ahead of me lie more than 2,000 miles of Appalachian trail on the way to its southern terminus on Springer Mountain in Georgia. With a beautiful 70-degree day down in the valley, the temperature on the Katahdin summit is 45 degrees.

Old Appalachian Trail sign on Cove Mountain near the Blue Ridge Parkway in Virginia.

Foreword

In 1990, my Seeing Eye dog, Orient, and I hiked the entire Appalachian Trail beginning in Georgia and ending after 2,160 miles at Mt. Katahdin, in Baxter State Park in north central Maine. Our trek took eight and a half months and it was a Christian witness mission sharing God's love with all those that we met along the way.

The most effective instrument among the thru-hikers is the information pipeline or rumor mill. When anything happens, good or bad, it is immediately transmitted to span the entire 2000 miles of the Appalachian Trail. During a week off the trail in Duncannon, PA, I heard of a young man called the Peacewalker, who was a south bounder also hiking as a Christian witness. For the next two months, I heard wonderful stories about this man. I heard how much he had wanted the opportunity to hike the Appalachian Trail for a period of over ten years. Through prayer, God enabled him to do so the same year that He sent me north bound for the same purpose.

It was a beautiful fall day in Vermont and both of us knew that we were going to meet that same day. When we did meet on the north side of Mount Killington, near Sherbourne Pass, it was as though we had known each other all our lives. We became fast and life-long friends at that moment, even though we were able to spend only a few minutes together at that time.

Since we met, we have spent a great deal of time together where we both had speaking engagements in nearby places and some quality time on the Appalachian Trail.

Ken Wadness, a.k.a. "Peacewalker", has written a wonderful book about his experience of the seven month sojourn on the Appalachian Trail.

It's not just an also-ran trail log of seven months of moaning and groaning about how painful it is to hike fifteen miles a day with sixty-five pounds on your back. Instead, it is a testimony of faith in God and expresses gratitude for the wonderful blessings God sent his way each day.

His ability to describe God's beautiful wilderness so vividly that while reading about it, one gets the sense of being there. This was surpassed by his talent for capturing these vivid scenes on film, many of which appear in the book.

I trust your life will be richer after reading Sojourn in the Wilderness and that it will instruct you, encourage you, and at the same time, challenge you to a closer walk with God so that you may reap a much richer harvest of grace, mercy, peace, and joy.

Bill Irwin
GA-ME 1990

The Knife's Edge on Mt. Katahdin, ME. I tried to begin my journey by ascending Mt. Katahdin along this route. Forty-five m.p.h. winds sent me back to Chimney Pond.

Walking Through the Northern Wilderness

Maine

My heart pounded as we passed through the ranger station into Baxter State Park. The long drive had given me plenty of time to think. I knew that only 10 percent of those who try to thru-hike the Appalachian Trail complete their journeys. People who quit give many different reasons for doing so. Like many of them, I was inexperienced; three weekend hikes in the White Mountains were the only true backpacking trips I had taken. How could I possibly do this formidable trek of 2,160 miles? This and other questions swirled through my mind as we drove the dirt road to the place in Katahdin Stream Campground that I had reserved four months earlier. From the summit of Mt. Katahdin the Appalachian Trail descends along a rock-strewn plateau called the Table Land, then down a steep rocky spur called The Gateway, to this campground. I planned to rest there for the night before beginning the greatest adventure of my life.

Setback with a Purpose

After setting up camp, I prepared my pack for a hike to and from the summit of Mt. Katahdin. This 5,267-foot peak is the highest in Maine. The following morning Sondra dropped me off at Roaring Brook Campground so I could walk the three miles into Chimney Pond. There I would connect with the Dudley Trail and begin my ascent of Pamola, a 4,900-foot peak connecting with Mt. Katahdin by a precipitous ridge called the Knife's Edge. This is the most difficult way up the mountain. Pamola was named after an

Katahdin Stream Falls near the Holt and Appalachian Trail after descending four miles from the top of Mt. Katahdin in Baxter State Park.

View of Mt. Katahdin near the Abol Deadwaters

Indian legend about the Great Spirit who dwelt on the fierce, wind-driven summit of Katahdin, a word that means "Greatest Mountain." I would learn first-hand the respect the Native Americans had for Pamola and the huge mountain next to it. The hike up Chimney Pond Trail was not strenuous. Containing only what I needed for this 10-mile round trip, my pack weighed about 25 pounds. As I climbed into the ravine containing the pond, the views I beheld of the giant head-walls surrounding it became grander. After checking in with the ranger, I drank from the pond and ceremoniously shaved off the mustache I had for more than 12 years. I decided not to shave or cut my hair until my journey was ended. After saying a prayer, I began climbing. It was cloudy and windy, the morning of July 3rd.

Ascending through an avalanche of boulders, the Dudley Trail goes up the Pamola head-wall. In many steep pitches of the trail, I needed to pull myself up by my hands. As I moved upward, the wind picked up. With each hundred feet in elevation gain, it seemed to double in strength, and as I neared the summit of Pamola, huge ripping gusts pushed me against rocks. At times I had to grab onto boulders to keep from falling. Knowing that the steeper Knife's Edge, with no protection from the wind, would be even more difficult, I began to feel afraid and thought of turning back. For a time I sat in a rocky crevice and cried a bit, wondering why this was all happening. I had felt sure that it was God's intention for me to hike the Appalachian Trail, and that this was the right time, but now, on the first day, I felt as though I was being sent back. Doubts plagued me as I began the arduous descent off Pamola and returned to Chimney Pond. In hiking back to Roaring Brook Campground, deep in thought, I tried to understand my predicament.

What I did not know then was that my brother Gary had driven to Baxter State Park to surprise me. While I was struggling on Pamola, he was hiking with Sondra up Mt. Katahdin from the other side, expecting to meet me at the summit. The wind in the Gateway and Table Land area was not as severe. Sondra went four miles up the mountain before turning around. Gary made the summit. By the time I hiked down to Roaring Brook Campground and hitched a ride to Katahdin Stream Campground, Sondra was there, at the campsite. I felt great disappointment and frustration in not having reached the top of Katahdin. Also, as darkness set in, I was beginning to worry about my brother, who had not returned.

Finally, at dusk, Gary and another couple came hiking down the trail and into the campground. It was wonderful to see my brother and learn of his successful ascent of Katahdin. I was truly sorry not to have met him on the summit. That evening in the campground I told Gary of my misadventures. Just after dinner a beautiful young bull moose walked within 20 feet of us. We watched it for about 10 minutes as it meandered down the campsite

Moose feeding in one of many ponds in Baxter State Park, ME.

Mt. Katahdin in Baxter State Park, ME is the northern terminus of the Appalachian Trail. Called "the greatest mountain" by the Abenaki Indians, it is 5,267 feet above sea level at its summit.

trail, nibbling on foliage – a promising ending to a day filled with emotional uncertainty.

That night in my tent, I entered "Day 1" in my journal and tried to write what I was thinking and feeling. *"Lord, what a test!* *Physically and mentally to ascend the mountain up to Knife's Edge..."* I paused, realizing that this experience would be a spiritual test as well. Eventually I came to see that God allowed the day to unfold in a way that helped me see within. My desire was to sense God more clearly and become a better person through this journey. *"God demonstrated his awesome power in nature today. I believe He sent a super-strong wind to stop my ascent. Why? I am not entirely sure. But standing on the edge of a trail as I was, fighting against a 50 m.p.h. wind, what could I do but sub-mit to Him and the power in nature? I felt humbled."*

Fresh Start

Awakening the next day to heavy clouds and a cold rain, I realized it would be impossible for me to try the climb again. A day of rest was actually welcome. The cool mist settled around Sondra and me as we said our fare-wells to Gary. Patience was the next lesson I learned. Hiking in that weather would have been foolish, so Sondra and I drove along the unpaved Perimeter Road, which rims the southern, western and northern sections of the park. Traveling slowly on that bumpy surface, we could relax and take in the park's vast beauty.

Baxter State Park was a gift to Maine from one of the state's former governors, the wonderful Percival Proctor Baxter. His vision, determination, and resources helped preserve more than 200,000 acres of mountain territory, wild forests and water sanctu-aries. A stone along the Appalachian Trail in Katahdin Stream Campground is fitted with a bronze plaque quoting Baxter: **"Man is born to die. His works are short-lived. Buildings crumble, mon-uments decay, wealth vanishes. But Katahdin and all its glory for-ever shall remain the mountain of the people of Maine."** With that thought in mind, Sondra and I explored the park for the rest of the day. At some level all the while, I was mentally preparing for the following day.

The Knife's Edge no longer captivated my imagination. It would have to wait until some future time, I decided, opting to climb Katahdin on the Abol Trail, which was a more direct route. The trail begins at Abol Campground, just a few miles from where I was camped; it then ascends steeply and precariously up the path of a cliff-destroying landslide that occurred in 1816. As I took to the trail the next morning, the weather was cool and clear – a pic-ture-perfect day. Along the way I met several people including another southbound thru-hiker, a Canadian named Steve whose trail name was Lord Mud. We talked of our hopes and separated before reaching the top of the mountain. I could not believe how the weather changed once I got up onto the Table Land, a relatively flat boulder-strewn area above timberline near the summit. The winds again picked up, and the temperature dropped dramatically – to about 40 or 45 degrees – but the sun was still shining in and out of passing clouds. Finally, in the afternoon, I reached the summit. As I stood on the highest mountain in Maine, I looked south and could see where my trek would take me, over many mountains and through many valleys.

At that moment I opened my journal. *"The excitement of starting this trip is also filled with much trepidation. Will I make it to Georgia? Who knows? It seems like a dream."* On the way up my primary focus had been the summit, but I also wanted to savor the process – the beauty and joy of nature combined with exhaustion and pain. Somehow, without knowing it, I had injured my left ankle on the climb and developed a huge blister at the back of my right heel. However, since my goal was not just to conquer the mountain or the journey but to learn and be changed by the experience, I needed to accept the discomfort. When I reached the base of the mountain on my way down, I was hobbling. After an ice-cold soaking in Katahdin Stream and a quiet dinner, I retired to my tent, exhausted and nervously anticipating the next day.

The 100-Mile Wilderness

After awakening early, I had difficulties and frustrations right away. Knowing I had too much in my pack had not stopped me from filling every conceivable crevice or from tying things on the outside of the pack, making it even heavier and more cumbersome. It tortured me to have to leave some things behind, even at that point. For example, I had bought a small Gitzo tripod just for this trek. Whenever I photographed nature, I used a tripod for longer shutter speeds and greater depth of field. I hated to leave the tripod as well as my 24mm lens behind, but I was forced to make weight-cutting concessions. The photo gear I kept with me consisted of a Nikon FE and 35-135 zoom lens, an 81A filter and a polarizing filter. As the packing process went into its frustrating third hour, I eliminated food and items of clothing. I thought I would never leave the campground that day.

Finally, after much toil, sweat and testing of my fragile patience, I was ready to depart. It was almost 11 a.m. The day was sunny and warm. Although the bulging pack still weighed more than 80 pounds, I hoisted it to my back, and tears welled up in my eyes as I said good-bye to Sondra and the comfortable life. Feeling the burden heavy upon my shoulders and waist, I slowly turned and

Hiking off the Tableland near Mt. Katahdin's rock strewn summit. White blazes begin guiding me on the long journey south.

Baxter State Park and the 100-Mile Wilderness as seen from the Holt Trail on Mt. Katahdin.

began to follow 2x6-inch white blazes. These trail indicators, painted on rocks, trees and telephone poles along the trail from Maine to Georgia, would become my constant guides. My labored steps were evident to anyone who saw me trudging along. The boot on my left foot was only half tied because of the intense pain it caused me if it was fully laced. My mind was filled with doubts. My heart felt heavy. My body struggled under the tremendous load. My pained feet could barely support me. The trail finally turned off into the woods toward the south, and my crossing of the 100-Mile Wilderness began.

I could no longer hold in the tears as I walked over rocks and roots and through bogs. Looking back on this initial misery, I can well understand how many hikers, after spending so much time and resources in preparing for an expedition like this, give up after a short time. For me at this point, the pain, combined with fear of the unknown, seemed too much to bear. As tears rolled down my cheeks, my prayers for strength, guidance and peace of mind ascended to God.

It was more than nine miles to my first campsite, Abol Bridge. When I finally arrived there, I felt exhausted but managed to set up my tent. The bridge crosses the West Branch of the Penobscot River, and there are tent sites near the shore below the structure. At this campsite I ran into Lord Mud again. His girl-friend planned to quit the trail the next morning, and I thought it would be good to have his company at the start of my journey. After a cold swim in the river, I retired early because hordes of black flies and mosquitoes were seeking an evening meal from me. *"The trail was relatively flat and followed along some beautiful rivers. The mosquitoes were horrible in many places. Even now as I write, the netting on my tent is covered with them and with tiny biting flies called no-see-ums. I wanted to quit a few times today. The pain in my left foot was excruciating. Actually, this was the most physically and emotionally painful day of my life."*

The following morning I was alone in the campsite, and it took me more than an hour to pack and have breakfast. Most of my breakfasts consisted of a handful or two of dry cereal, a granola bar and a vitamin-fortified powdered drink (chocolate) used by people who are dieting. My mom's boss, from Health Management Resources, let me use his company's drink supplement and extra vit-amins for energy on the trail. Vitamin depravation can be a prob-lem with long-distance hikers since they burn more than 5,000 calories each day. On some mornings I heated water for instant oatmeal. I did not do this often, however, because I wanted to con-serve fuel and get early starts on the trail.

Once packed, I left Abol Bridge, hobbling. Again, the only way I could stand the pain in my left ankle was to have the laces of my left boot tied half way up. It was a beautiful summer day with temperatures in the 80s. That is wonderful at the beach, but in the

Steve, Troy, Shannon and I stopped for lunch on Rainbow Lake's eastern shore.

Eastern shore of Rainbow Lake in the 100-Mile Wilderness.

northern Maine wilderness it can be a problem, for I sweat heavily, and by noon the perspiration running down my shirt, shorts and legs had soaked my boots. Also, with swarms of mosquitoes and black flies in the air, it was next to impossible to stop and rest without being fiercely attacked. I caught up with Steve after hiking two miles and came to Hurd Brook Lean-to, the first shelter on the northern end of the Appalachian Trail. A shelter on the trail is usually a three-sided wooden structure with a platform that can accommodate from six to ten people.

At Hurd Brook, Steve and I met two other southbound hikers, Troy and Shannon, from Indiana. One of these men was planning to hike at least half the trail to West Virginia. The other was planning to go to Georgia. They were hiking very slowly and seemed to have more gear than I had. Each carried three knives and unneeded army paraphernalia. They had already taken an extra day off in the 100-Mile Wilderness, and I had no idea how they were going to make it without running out of food. The four of us hiked together most of day to the next shelter. It was great to have someone along to provide encouragement when I became weak and weary. Unfortunately, I had to switch from my boots to the pair of sneakers after only five miles of hiking that day because the pain in my left foot became even more severe. Walking over roots and rocks and in mud is challenging enough in heavy boots, but with sneakers and an 80-pound pack it is trying. Still, it was good that I had the sneakers because I could not have continued in boots.

The trail took us over the beautiful and rocky Rainbow Ledges and then back down to Rainbow Lake. At a picturesque opening in the trees at the southeast end of the lake, we stopped to have lunch. I shared part of a two-pound block of cheddar cheese, and this helped lighten my load. (Most of my trail lunches consisted of peanut butter and jelly on either bread, English muffins or bagels. Blocks of cheddar or cream cheese would hold up pretty well for many days even in the summer heat. For a change, I carried one or two cans of tuna. At times I would snack on cookies, peanut M&Ms or beef jerky.) The trail meandered over countless rocks and roots along the five-mile shoreline of this beautiful body of water that can be reached only by air or foot travel. Birds and water-fowl filled the breezes with delightful melodies.

After leaving the lake, we came to the Rainbow Stream Lean-to, where I had my first stay in an Appalachian Trail shelter. Having struggled the last few of 14 and a half miles, I collapsed on the floor. Then, after taking a cool dip in the stream, I ate a delicious noodle dinner – with some dehydrated vegetables thrown in – and felt better. All trail dinners needed to be boiled, and I rotated through macaroni and cheese, spaghetti, scalloped and au gratin potatoes, rice pilafs, wild grain rice, and various Lipton soups and

Near the summit of Nesuntabunt Mountain overlooking Nahmakanta Lake with Mt. Katahdin and Baxter State Park in the distance.

noodle or rice dinners. To every one of these meals I added squeezes of margarine and dehydrated potatoes, vegetables or hamburger. On cooler evenings I started with a cup of soup or hot chocolate.

As I snuggled into my sleeping bag in the lean-to, I was bone weary and sore. After reading for a time in my Bible, I wrote in my journal. *"I am learning a lot of patience out here. It is good to have support from friends when I am hiking in pain and finding the way difficult. I thank God for the strength He gave me today, and I praise Him for this wonderful place and His peace."*

Maine

"Birds and water-fowl filled the breezes with delightful melodies."

A Routine Established

Trying to awaken early on the longest days of the year is difficult. My body was always sore from the previous day's trials. Steve was invariably the first to leave a shelter. Shannon and Troy usually resumed hiking hours after the sun came up and after I had left. As I left Rainbow Stream and worked my way through the rich green forests on Nesuntabunt Mountain, a beautiful day was upon me. Alas, so were pesky insects. Nesuntabunt, which is 35 miles by trail from Mt. Katahdin but only 15 as the eagle flies, has magnificent views of the Greatest Mountain and the southern part of Baxter State Park. Again, sneakers replaced boots – this time after only four miles of hiking.

When I caught up with Steve, he was not hiking fast but seemed to be wandering through the woods. Approaching him, I saw a frightened look on his face. He had been spooked by something in the woods, so we hiked together for the rest of the day. We rested long on top of Nesuntabunt, enjoying breathtaking views, and Wadleigh Stream Lean-to was an easy two miles down the other side of the mountain. We hung around the empty shelter for awhile debating whether we should stay in the mosquito- and black fly-infested forest there or camp on the small beach of Nahmakanta Lake a half mile away. The choice was easy. Shannon and Troy rolled into the shelter just as Steve and I were leaving for the lake. They looked exhausted. I knew they did not have enough food to make it through the 100-Mile Wilderness, and they already seemed resigned to give up. They would not consider hiking a half mile farther that day to a peaceful lakeside spot for the night. As we parted, I wondered if we would ever see them again – and in fact we did not.

Steve and I set up our tents in the sand and took a dip in the cool, placid lake before dinner. As the sun began to set, we were attacked by no-see-ums. Their sharp, unrelenting stings were so awful that we had to jump into our tents. After zipping the netting quickly, I sat and scratched my body for five minutes. Then, using a flashlight in the waning light of day, I hunted and exterminated bugs in the tent. (To ensure a peaceful rest, I went through a similar ceremony every night of the summer.) When I got out of the tent to relieve myself that night, I almost screamed from the pain of thousands of tiny creatures biting all at once. I received more than 25 bites in less than a minute, and my legs burned after I got back to the tent, which I entered on the run. Shining my head lamp out from the inside, I saw that the mesh door was plastered with insects. *"Thank God for no-see-um netting!"* That night, when I heard the enchanting melody of loons calling to each other across the lake, I felt a stirring in my soul. Unable to sleep, I wrote this...

I hear the sweet, lonely call of the majestic loon
And listen intently to her ancient, mighty tune.
My open heart leaps with enraptured wonder and joy,
Bringing back age-old memories of when I was a boy.

Royal melodies fill my spirit with profound expectancy,
As if in this eerie darkness I have just begun to see.
Hearing her piercing wail echo throughout this peaceful,
    calm lake.
Such a precious difference only one solitary voice can make.

My heart is opened to hear the Lord's still, quiet voice
When He speaks: I praise Him and greatly rejoice.
I'm now filled with His sweet gentle Spirit, and
    peace besides,
All the while pondering the precious gifts He has
    placed inside.

Steve (Lord Mud) and I camped on this beautiful sandy beach at Lower Jo-Mary Lake.

Sinking Puncheons

"When I awoke in the night to the sound of rain, I had to run out of my tent and quickly put my rain-fly over it. I was bitten more than a dozen times just putting the tarp on. When Steve left in the morning, it was pouring. I prayed that the rain would ease up so I could get going — I did not want to start out in a downpour. Well, when I finally got out of my tent, the rain had just about stopped. I couldn't believe it!"

That day's fairly flat trail followed the beautiful Nahmakanta Stream. It was boggy in many spots, and I fell four times. Two falls were especially hard because I was making my way over slippery old puncheons — bridges usually made from one or two cut trees raised at both ends above the marshy earth. At one point the trail was so water-logged that for a short distance hikers had taken an alternate route. I was having a difficult time with the

Maine

boggy mess, so I decided to take the side trail. What a mistake! Seldom used, this path had even older puncheons lying in even wetter bogs. Also, the mosquitoes and black flies were about the worst I had seen. Stopping to rest brought them in a fury around my sweating face, neck, arms and legs.

When I came to a swampy area with half-submerged puncheons, I wondered how anyone could pass through there, but I began to traverse the unstable bridges, carefully balancing myself with my hiking staff. I made it over two 15-foot puncheons and half way across a third when suddenly my right foot began to slip off the partially submerged timber. The weight of my pack sent my unbalanced body reeling forward, and my foot sank into the slimy mud to mid-thigh. The rest of me smashed down on the log. My sweaty face came to rest in thick muck and mire. Stunned and motionless, I lay on my stomach with the pack pressing against my back and mud beginning to seep into my clothes. The log was now submerged in warm, foul-smelling water, and hundreds of hungry insects swarmed around me. It took me several minutes and a number of tries to get out of that mess. It took longer to get some of the sludge off my body and out of my drenched boot. But I worked as quickly as I could. Right then, as I sat there by the trail, deep doubt about the wisdom of this journey seeped into my mind. It was a low and dark moment for me as I contemplated this walk of more than 2,000 miles, with its pain and frustration already so great. The idea of leaving the trail weaved in and out of my thoughts over the next few days.

Walking again, I passed through more boggy areas and then noticed a yellow figure moving ahead of me. In 90-degree heat it was strange to see, but as I caught up with the figure, I saw that it was Steve and that he had put his rain poncho over his head and pack to keep off the insects. He told how slow-going the day had been for him and how he hoped I would catch up. Earlier he had seen a bear in the woods. I told him I had heard a moose crashing through woods about 50 yards ahead of me, but I never saw it. Later that day we met our first north-bound thru-hiker. He called himself the Connecticut Yankee and was dressed head-to-toe in wool. This was oppressively hot, but it was his way of fighting the insatiable insects. Because of the insects we could talk to him for only a short while before moving on.

In the late afternoon we arrived at the next shelter, Potaywadjo Spring Lean-to. Although it was near a beautiful 20-foot wide spring that flowed with clear, cold bubbling water, we decided not to stay there. The insect population was just too dense, and the map told us of a sandy beach a mile and a half from the shelter along the shores of Lower Jo-Mary Lake, which we hoped would be as lovely as the Nahmakanta Lake beach. We hiked down the trail and were filled with delight as we came out of the insect-infested forest onto a magnificent, breezy white sandy beach at the end of a peaceful lake.

"The weight of my pack sent my unbalanced body reeling forward, and my foot sank into the slimy mud to mid-thigh."

"While we were setting up our tents, two loons floated by and called to each other four times. It was God sent. I later took a refreshing swim in this pristine mountain lake. The sky was clearing, and the sun was slowly setting. Now, as I sit peacefully in this wilderness paradise, 50 feet behind me are the woods with its torture chamber of black flies and mosquitoes — a million of them! Earlier today I prayed that my boots would last until the next shelter or campsite because the terrain was so rough on my feet. I had previously been able to hike only three to five miles in my boots until the pain became unbearable, especially in my injured left ankle. I made it all the way to the shelter and past it by about two miles! Eleven and a half miles, in one day, in my boots! Through the intense heat, in falling off slippery roots, fighting off swarms of insects and at times in great pain, I came to feel that God was teaching me to slow down in life. Gradually, I was learning what it would mean to be a Peacewalker and see life's circumstances in a different way. At the start of the day, I was thinking of hiking 20 miles. Why? I would have missed out on the blessing of sitting here in this oasis, away from the heat and bugs. God does answer prayer. I pray that I will continue to grow stronger, and that tomorrow I will take my time. No more walking my own way through the wilderness — only God's ways."

Blisters

The next morning, Steve and I meandered along the edge of Lower Jo-Mary for almost two miles, then came onto a bog-filled logging road. I almost ran out of water as the high heat and humidity drained the moisture and energy from my body. In the heat of summer, I measured a mountain's difficulty by how many quarts of water I had to consume in climbing it. For some mountains, if the next spring or stream was too far away, I needed to carry three quarts of water. Resulting from the stiffness of my boots and the moisture from my sweat and the muddy trail, my feet had painful blisters. Constant pain was keeping my mileage down and my faith in God up. After hiking almost 10 miles with little elevation gain along this boggy section of trail, Steve and I came to Cooper Brook Lean-to, which has a peaceful waterfall and natural pool. From there the trail leaves the lower elevation of the northern Maine woods and rises into the next mountain range. The 11 and a half miles of trail to Logan Spring Lean-to, at an elevation of 2,250 feet, wind over Little Board Man Mountain and then half way up White Cap Mountain. Here the path passes under many "blow-downs," trees that have fallen and have not yet been cleared from the trail. I wrote in my journal that night.

"It was a good day walking — just taking my time, talking and singing to God. The valleys in the wilderness and those in my life can be very hard places to be in, just like the low areas of the Maine woods with the heat, bugs and bogs. I'd rather be hiking up on the mountains, but they present their own kind of pain and difficulty. I am beginning to learn, though, that many of life's most precious lessons are learned in moving to and from mountain tops, with God revealing Himself in special ways along the way."

Maine

Blow-Downs

Two exhausted men calling themselves the Myers Brothers pulled into the Logan Spring shelter around 8 p.m. They had just "flipped-flopped" on the trail. Flip-flopping is hiking a section of trail, then leaving it at a predetermined end point and being driven to another part of the trail to hike back to that point. These men had hiked all the way from Georgia to West Virginia, then had been driven to Mt. Katahdin and were now hiking south, back to West Virginia. They were funny characters reputed to be expert "blue-blazers." A blue-blazer is a hiker who substitutes a blue-blazed side trail for the white-blazed Appalachian Trail. Some side trails that come back to the main trail can make the hike in certain sections easier and shorter. That evening the Myers Brothers decided not to continue south on the white-blazed Appalachian Trail but to blue-blaze some of the 100-Mile Wilderness so they would not have to traverse the next four mountains in the White Cap Mountain Range. Lord Mud decided to join them.

Early the next morning, after saying good-bye to the newly formed threesome of hikers, I left the shelter on a trail that turned upward toward the 3,644-foot main peak of White Cap Mountain. The trail then went gruelingly over Hay Mountain and West Peak. In many places the path looked as if it had not been touched in years and was so overgrown with spruce trees that I could hardly see it. Also, I counted 40 blow-downs in a one-mile section. I had to take off my pack and crawl under many of them, pulling the pack along. In this manner I could make only six and a half miles that day, so I stopped at the Carl A. Newhall Lean-to. As I set up my gear there, I thought I would be alone for the first night in my trail experience. Soon, though, a Boy Scout troop from Calais, Maine came into the campsite. While listening to their noisy laughter, I wrote about sitting on Hog Mountain that day after hiking through many blow-downs. I had noticed how life and death are in balance in the natural world. Where there is a dead tree, a new one grows. Dead trees become the food and soil for new ones. I thought about my spiritual life that way. *"As I grow and change, I imagine my old nature dying within me and a new person emerging."*

Trillium on the Appalachian Trail in the 100-Mile Wilderness, White Cap Mountain, ME.

Resting at Cooper Brook in the 100-Mile Wilderness.

Thirst

The next day, as I walked through the Gulf Hagas Wilderness, was glorious. Known as the "Grand Canyon of the East," the gulf was formed by the eroding power of the West Branch of the Pleasant River running over slate. The canyon is three miles long, and the river, surrounded by many steep cliffs, drops 500 feet in elevation through many magnificent waterfalls. One of the most beautiful of these, Screw Auger Falls, is only a short distance off the Appalachian Trail. The 26-foot plunge

Climbing White Cap Mountain in Maine, with Mt. Katahdin in the distance. As the
trail's northern end receded in the distance, I found myself walking alone in the vast

has created a deep pool that is wonderful for swimming. It was hard for me to leave this area, but heading further south brought me to a woodland gem called the Hermitage, a forest containing a rare stand of white "King's pine," some of which were 130 feet tall. This forest is under the protection of the Nature Conservancy as a natural and historical resource, for in colonial times the trees were used for the masts of sailing ships and warships.

Crossing the West Branch of the Pleasant River can be dangerous, so I wore sneakers and used my staff. Beyond this point the trail advanced steeply up into the Barren Chairback Mountain Range, where there had been no rain for some time, and small streams and springs were drying up. *"Today was a hard day for me. The four-mile climb up Chairback Mountain was extremely exhausting. I got winded in the heat and felt I had no energy. As I sat on the summit, I saw a vast green wilderness and more than 50 peaks. I came into Chairback Shelter thinking this would be my first night alone, but I was wrong again. Tonight, I am sleeping in a shelter with eight girls from Camp Alford Lake. It is hard to imagine 11-year-olds camping out in the 100-Mile Wilderness. The spring was muddy and almost dry. After skimming muck off the top, I could get at the inch of water that lay beneath it."*

As I continued in the Chairback Range the next day, I ran out of water and slowly became dehydrated. Near the top of a ridge, though, I found a tiny slow-flowing spring with clear cold water. It took almost a half an hour to fill my three water bottles, but that spring was a life saver. That night I wrote in my journal. *"I believe I am totally alone tonight for the first time. After eleven and a half hard miles up and down four peaks — Columbus Mountain, Third Mountain, Fourth Mountain, and Barren Mountain at 2,670 feet — I decided I could not make it to the next lean-to. Long Pond Stream Lean-to was another six-tenths of a mile off the trail. I could go no farther when I got to the trail leading to it. As I stumbled down the Appalachian Trail, which followed Long Pond Stream, I noticed a small sandbar next to a beautiful waterfall. Hallelujah! The spot was just right for my tent. I could not hike to the end of this day if God were not with me, and now He has blessed me by letting me camp in this beautiful place. I am about seven feet from the water's edge and have just returned from a glorious swim. It is a clear night as I can see the stars shining through the netting on top of my tent."* While listening to the river flow endlessly by my tent that night, I penned this poem.

DOWN BY THE RIVER

> Down by the river God reveals Himself
> As our protector in our nightly slumber,
> As our provider when we need sustenance.
> His Spirit flows eternally and freely towards us
> To give new life to all who open their hearts.
> God's voice resounds like the rushing waters
> Waiting to be heard over all the earth.

Life giving spring water pours slowly into my water bottle on the ridge of the very dry Chairback Mountain Range in Maine. Most of the time I drank water straight from springs and high mountain streams. I used iodine and boiling to purify low-lying water.

Unable to make it to Long Pond Stream Lean-To one day, I camped by Slugundy Gorge and Falls in the 100-Mile Wilderness.

Maine

His gentle presence is felt in the cool mist of a
    new day.
God's gentle presence touches us in the early light,
His light shimmers on the ever flowing waters.
God's awesome light emanates from the
    lofty heavens,
His majestic glory radiates as the darkness
    slowly dissipates.
God is always here with us!

The weather kept getting hotter, the temperature soaring into the 90s with the humidity just as high. I was pushing myself beyond exhaustion and almost did not make it to Lehman Brook Lean-to. Stinging deer flies circled my head for more than 10 miles. My body became drenched with perspiration often on this 12-mile day, while most of the time I was out of drinking water and could find none. At one point after a series of steep hills, I collapsed. Feeling as if I was having heat stroke, I cried to God for water. I then got up and came down into a dried pond area and in walking around some boulders noticed a slight glimmer under a rock. There was only an inch and a half of standing water, but using my pan I got a quart and a half of water from that small hole – and it was cold and delicious! God answered my prayer.

"Today was the greatest test so far. I had no water for the last three miles before I got to the shelter. I collapsed a number of times from heat exhaustion on the trail because I couldn't go on. It took me more than 12 hours to hike 12 miles, and once I got to the shelter, all I could do was thank God. Nevertheless, I was still so hot and thirsty that I had to get down to Lehman Brook, about 150 feet downhill from the shelter, to cool off and obtain water. Once there, I sat in the stream and didn't move a muscle. While horrendous deer flies buzzed around my head, a swarm of mosquitoes came roaring in, so even though the temperature is in the 80s, I have set up my tent in the shelter so I can get a good night's rest. By now I have little food left for the seven-mile trek to the road that will lead me to Monson, Maine, my first trail town. Today on the trail, though, I got to pick my first blueberries, so I will use them in my last pancake mix for breakfast. It took me 12 days to hike the 100-Mile Wilderness, whereas I had planned to do it in ten. I have loved this wilderness and will truly miss it. Between yesterday and today I have not seen anyone, and I'm still alone. Yet I know God is here and has watched over me. I know I would have died today without that water from under the rock."

Screw Augur Falls, Gulf Hagas Wilderness, ME. This wilderness area contains a three-mile gorge known as the "Grand Canyon of the East." The gulf area can be seen by walking a five-mile loop off the Appalachian Trail.

Taking a swim in Long Pond Stream after a long day's hike.

WANDERING IN THE WILDERNESS

Wandering in the wilderness sheds light upon my
    thirsty soul,
While each new day's glorious inspiration makes me whole.
Walking with Almighty God can change my eternal
    perspective,

A "blow-down" is a tree that has fallen across the trail. This one is on Gulf Hagas Mountain in Maine's 100-Mile Wilderness. On certain sections of the trail, there were more than 40 blow-downs in a mile. Many were in such thick forest that the only way I could continue along the trail was to crawl on my stomach under the toppled trees.

Maine

Gulf Hagas Brook, Gulf Hagas Wilderness, ME. Hikers
must cross most streams in Maine without the benefit of
bridges. In high water most of these streams are waist-deep.

Ferns along the Appalachian Trail in the 100-Mile Wilderness, West Peak, ME.

With radiant eyes I see more clearly the life I need to
fully live.
Who needs to fear? Just take the first step and see,
When my life is yielded to God's gentle hands, I am
truly free.

Civilization

The pancakes stuck to my stomach like lead but gave me energy for the last seven gut-wrenching miles. When at last I was walking down the old farm road into Monson, tears of joy came to my eyes and rolled down my cheeks. I made it the two miles to a boarding house where I was met by the legendary Keith and Pat Shaw. The friendly Shaws have welcomed thousands of hikers to their home over the years, feeding them unbelievable meals. While I was there, Keith told a lot about Maine and shared some of his war experiences. At the house I met a northbound hiker named The Void, who bought six loaves of bread at a country store for his hike north through the 100-Mile Wilderness. He squeezed them into his pack. Later that day, Jeff (The Lummox) pulled in quite sick. He would not stay in the house because he did not want to get anyone else sick, so he camped on the lawn. Betty (The Geritol Dropout), who was also staying at Shaw's, taught me how to grip the frame of my pack from behind and flip it over my head. I used this method of putting on the pack most of the time after this.

To recuperate and rest up for what was ahead, I needed to spend an extra night at Shaw's. Keith served all-you-can-eat dinners and breakfasts, which helped me regain strength. He told me of a thru-hiker who in one sitting ate 20-plus eggs, many pieces of bacon and lots of helpings of home fries, vanquishing a previous "pig-out" record. He paid a price – keeled over on the floor, in pain for hours, and had to stay in bed for days before he fully recovered. Keith drove his son and me to the local beach where we swam for part of the afternoon. I then played horseshoes with Keith, and he beat me, of course. When I left the following morning after another filling breakfast, my pack weighed 67 pounds.

The hike to Moxie Bald Lean-to was not too bad. I followed the Piscataquis River and Bald Mountain Stream for nine miles, fording twice, and reached the shelter after hiking 15 miles – my longest day with a full pack. As it began to get dark, The Lummox and a hiker named Bill (Cougartail) arrived. They had left Shaw's that morning. It was great to have company again. We left in the morning and climbed two and a half miles to the summit of Moxie Bald Mountain, which is 2,630 feet high. Then we hiked by Joe's Hole Brook Lean-to and began the arduous four and a half mile ascent of Pleasant Pond Mountain. Still unaccustomed to the

"The trail to Caratunk offered us so many delicious raspberry patches that our appetites were satisfied by the time we arrived."

weight of my pack, I found it hard to climb any peak without running out of steam. The descent to Pleasant Pond Lean-to was only a mile but extremely steep. Fortunately, the lean-to had been fixed the day before – a tree had recently fallen on it. We had a great swim but poor sleep. Buzzing mosquitoes bothered us all night.

Maine

River-Crossing

We left early the next morning to get to Caratunk, Maine, so we could cross the Kennebec River. This was the most dangerous river-crossing on the Appalachian Trail. Hikers could ford the river only in the early morning when the water was waist deep – before an upstream dam released its flow for the day. There was free ferry service during the hiking season, but only for a few hours each day. In 1985 a hiker died trying to cross the river, and many more have been washed downstream with the loss of much gear. The trail to Caratunk offered us so many delicious raspberry patches that our appetites were satisfied by the time we arrived.

Caratunk is a quaint, one-store hamlet of about a hundred people. We arrived the day before their 150th-year celebration, which featured a parade, horseshoe contest and chicken supper. We were invited to stay and did not want to miss the event, but we left the town in the rain and headed down to the shores of the swift-moving river. There we met a great fellow named Steve who canoed each of us across. It took us half an hour to accomplish this. Beyond that for three and a half miles, the trail followed beautiful Pierce Pond Stream, its dozens of cascading waterfalls descending into the Kennebec River. When we arrived at Pierce Pond Lean-to, it was raining, and five northbound thru-hikers were in residence. Although there was room for us, they said they were waiting for friends to arrive and that we could hike to the next shelter, an "easy" 10 miles down the trail. Jeff, Bill, and I were trail-weary and unhappy at the thought of leaving this spot. With all the roots and rough terrain around the shelter, though, there seemed to be no place for tents, especially in the rain, so we reluctantly headed for West Carry Pond Lean-to.

"What a miraculous day, and I'm alive to tell about it! After hiking the ten miles to Pierce Pond, we had to go another ten to this new shelter. The trail was boggy and wet, but fairly flat in places. Still, I almost did not make it. Twenty miles in one day was too much for my system. I was hobbling when we arrived. My feet, especially the arches, had been hurting when we got to Pierce Pond. Now I can hardly walk. One of the three hikers in the lean-to, Jack, graciously helped me set up my tent. As I limped down to the pond to clean up, the storm started to clear away, the sun's golden rays turning fiery orange behind the clouds. Blisters formed in wet boots on today's forced march are almost down to the bone on the backs of my heels."

Steve (The Void) and all his hiking gear on the Shaw's lawn.

I stayed two nights with Jeff (The Lummox) and Betty (The Geritol Dropout) at Shaw's Boarding House.

"when we awoke the following morning, we knew we could not hike and decided that a day's rest was needed for our feet, bodies and spirits."

When we awoke the following morning, we knew we could not hike and decided that a day's rest was needed for our feet, bodies and spirits. Blessed with a gorgeous day, we relaxed and swam in the pond – a pause that helped heal our aching bodies. The idea of taking a Sabbath Day's rest came to me as I sat in prayer beside that beautiful pond. As a thru-hiker, my tendency, I realized, could be to look at the ground and keep moving all the time. The goal of finishing the hike would then be more important than the whole process of getting there. I still needed to learn to slow my pace. Jeff and I left Bill at the shelter the next morning because he had decided that this was it for his southbound journey. The seven miles to Little Bigelow Lean-to were not too difficult. Jeff and I arrived there in the early afternoon and decided to stay. It is a delightful place called "The Tubs," where cold water runs into two pools in the brook. It was refreshing to be there and a blessing to have Jeff along in this part of my walk. *"God has shown me how important friends are in life. They help in times of difficulty, give encouragement when you're down, and are willing to carry your burdens if necessary."*

When we left the shelter to climb the two miles to the summit of Little Bigelow Mountain, it was raining hard. It was a good hard climb up Little Bigelow and much harder up Bigelow Mountain, which included Avery Peak at 4,088 feet, West Peak at 4,150 feet and South Horn at 3,381 feet. Climbing my first 4,000-footer in the rain was quite an experience. The clouds swirled around the mountain, and the wind was blowing hard by the time we reached Avery Peak. Jeff and I were cold and wet as we ate lunch in a lean-to in the col between the peaks, and because this shelter provided little protection from the storm, we quickly ascended West Peak, descended the Horns and climbed down to the Horns Pond Lean-tos. One of those shelters was filled with an Outward Bound group. The other we shared with two Chicagoans. (Interestingly, waste from the nearby privy is dried by solar-panel heat and then spread on the forest floor as fertilizer.) We spent a cool, wet night in the shelter. It had a small leak in the roof, which I repaired by tying rope at the leak and stretching it to the ground outside. The water, following the rope, did not drip on us all night. That night I prayed. *"May God pour out His Spirit upon me as He pours this needed rain upon the parched land. As the rain seeps into the wells that lie within the mountains, let the rain of the Holy Spirit fill my inner well so I can give from it to others."*

Jeff and I left the shelter early, hiked five miles down to Route 27 and headed into Stratton to get our next mail and food. We tried to hitch into town, but no one picked us up until we had walked three and a half miles. We were dropped off at the Widow's Walk Bed & Breakfast by a nice lady driving a pickup. We then did our laundry, got our mail, and went to the store. Sondra, who had waited for us at the trail crossing but missed us, later treated us to a great dinner out. My re-supplied pack weighed more than 70 pounds – way too much.

Maine

Crossing a bog on a "puncheon," a split log used as a foot-bridge, near the West Branch of the Piscataquis River in Maine.

West Carry Pond Lean-to. Cougar Tail, The Lummox and I spent two nights at this shelter to help heal the deep blisters on our feet. Cougar Tail decided to end his southbound journey.

Sunset on West Carry Pond. "From the rising of the sun unto the going down of the same, the name of the Lord is to be praised." (Psalm 113:3)

Mushrooms next to the trail on Bigelow Mountain.

This is the "Big Tub" in the ice-cold stream near Little Bigelow Lean-to.

Maine

The following morning Sondra drove Jeff and me back to the trail, and the two of us toiled up Crocker Mountain, taking more than three hours to reach the North Peak at 4,168 feet. After lunch we hiked over to the South Peak and negotiated the steep rocky descent to Crocker Cirque Campsite. There we met a couple from Connecticut who were finishing the final leg of their hike on the Appalachian Trail. They had hiked over three summers and would end their journey in Hanover, New Hampshire. Hob and Deb called themselves The Tandem Teachers because they are elementary school teachers and have ridden a tandem bicycle in many places around the world. We had a great time talking while camped on tent platforms under the stars next to a babbling brook.

In the morning we all descended to the base of Sugarloaf Mountain and met a famous thru-hiker named Second Wind, who had done the whole trail five times. Later in the day we met Inward Bound from Connecticut. The Sugarloaf climb was steep. It was a lovely fair-weather day, however, and we decided to take a half-mile side trail to the 4,237-foot summit – the highest in this section of Maine. The trail then climbed over Spalding Mountain at 3,988 feet on the way to Spalding Mountain Lean-to.

Mountain Top Experiences

For some prayer time I wanted to spend the night alone on Mount Abraham but decided instead to leave the shelter at 3 a.m. and meet the rising sun on the summit. I actually left about 4 o'clock and walked by head lamp for an hour, making it to the chilly 4,043-foot summit before sunrise and spending four to five hours in peaceful prayer and praise by the time Hob, Deb, and Jeff joined me. The sunrise was a precious time for me as I watched the sun slowly rise over the horizon and felt God's awesome peace descend upon the mountaintop.

The trail from there descended more than 2,000 vertical feet in six miles to Orbeton Stream, which can be a dangerous crossing at high water. We had a wonderful rest and swim, not realizing how steep and tough the climb up Poplar Ridge, on the other side of the stream, would be. We made it to Poplar Ridge Lean-to in the late afternoon, hot and sweaty. This shelter still had a "baseball bat" style sleeping platform – the surface made of small trees, not wooden planks, so when you slept, you felt the ridges massaging your aching back.

Leaving Poplar Ridge, we began our climb over the Saddleback Range with three distinct peaks: Saddleback Junior, The Horn, and Saddleback Mountain at 4,116 feet. We were blessed with magnificent weather in this walk through pristine country and were above timberline for more than three miles. A small bump that we could see on the horizon to the northeast was

"The sunrise was a precious time for me as I watched the sun slowly rise over the horizon and felt God's awesome peace descend upon the mountaintop."

Mt. Katahdin. As we moved along, we saw the glory of God's creation and were reluctant to leave the Saddleback summit. At last we made our way down the four miles to the Piazza Rock Lean-to and tent platforms, where many hikers were camping for the day because the facility is fairly close to a major road.

As we hiked 10 miles to the next shelter, Sabbath Day Pond Lean-to, I became more convinced of my need to take a Sabbath Day's rest each week I spent in the wilderness. With our equipment set up in the lean-to, we took a short walk north on the Appalachian Trail to beautiful Long Pond and swam in it, agreeing that this was the best beach we had seen so far. I was awakened at 4:45 in the morning by splashing in the water near the lean-to. A moose was eating in the pond. This was a pleasant surprise before the morning light began to fill the forest, waking all the birds and their friends. After an early start we climbed into the Bemis Mountain Range, traversing the First Peak and Second Peak and arriving at Bemis Mountain Lean-to, where we met northbound thru-hikers The Archer and Polyester in mid-afternoon. It was relaxing to get to a shelter early. We could set up for the night, get dinner ready and, best of all, talk to other hikers, sharing stories and enjoying the scenery while it was still light. *"'How pleasant it is,' the Bible says, 'when brethren dwell together in unity.' This is true.'"*

We left the shelter early in the morning and headed south again as most other hikers were continuing north. It was only a mile and a half to the rocky summit of 3,532-foot Bemis Mountain, where we had to find shelter from harsh winds that drove white clouds rapidly across the sky overhead. The trail then meandered along the ridge to Old Blue Mountain, bringing the beautiful mountains of western Maine into view. Our descent off Old Blue was steep, and then we climbed the infamous Moody Mountain. When many sections of the trail were made in Maine, only a few switch backs were put in; the trail usually went straight up or down a mountain. Moody is a classic example. Although the summit is only 2,350 feet above sea level, the trail drops more than 1,100 feet in less than a mile to Sawyer Brook. The pounding from this walk left my knees in pain by the end of the day. Sawyer Brook flows between Moody and Wyman Mountains, which ascend dramatically on both sides of a magnificent narrow valley reminiscent of Yosemite in California – minus the crowds. Hob, Deb, Jeff and I decided to camp there instead of making the one-mile climb to Hall Mountain Lean-to, on the ridge of Wyman Mountain.

In the morning I found the steep ascent to the lean-to to be even more demanding than the climb up Moody. The hike over Wyman Mountain, cresting at 2,945 feet, was cold and accompanied by heavy drizzle and fog. We moved on as quickly as we could, coming down to East B Hill Road where we hoped to hitch into Andover, our next trail town. Unbelievably, within five minutes three guys let all four of us cram into the back of their pickup

for the eight-mile ride. They dropped us off at the Andover Arms Bed & Breakfast, which run by Pat and Larry and where for five dollars a night hikers can stay in a barn attached to the house. Pat and Larry were gracious hosts and fed us well. After a breakfast feast Pat drove us back up to the trail, and we began our long ascent of Baldpate Mountain. Beyond Frye Notch Lean-to, surprisingly, we met some of the Camp Alford Lake girls I had seen three weeks earlier in the 100-Mile Wilderness. Baldpate's treeless summits, East Peak at 3,812 feet and West Peak at 3,680 feet, were magnificent to walk upon. As we sat on the windless top of East Peak enjoying a wonderful lunch, beautiful cumulus clouds floated overhead in a brilliant blue sky. It was hard to leave this scene and walk off into the valley. Pat picked us up at Grafton Notch and drove us back to the Andover Arms for more food, fun and fellowship.

We all decided to take an extra day off when Hob's brother Jay came to visit us in Andover. He took us for a drive to Coos Canyon, where we swam among the smooth rocks and rapids. We also drove to Camp Wai-ai-we on Gull Pond and sailed in a great wind for most of the afternoon. We were treated to the sight of a huge moose strutting gracefully along the rocky shoreline. After a splendid cookout with scrumptious raspberry pie for dessert, we retired early in the camp's comfy cabins, awakening at 4 a.m. for a pre-dawn canoe ride on the Kennebago River near Rangely. As we began our paddle down the river, a thick mist floated around us and covered the tranquil countryside in this vast wilderness. The sun rose slowly over the horizon, trying to break through the mist. This gave the meandering river such a glorious glow that I felt God surrounding us with His glory and peace. An hour later, when we came upon a mama moose and her calf feeding in the river, we slowed to a stop, silently transfixed at the precious scene until the animals wandered back into the forest.

Hiking along the open ridge of the Saddleback Mountain Range, ME.

By the time we got back to Andover that morning, its Old Home Fair was in full progress. Thousands of people descended upon the town for this event. I could not stay for all the festivities because I was going to meet my folks at Larry and Mary's house in Albany. Over the years this couple had acquired land for a home and created a small wilderness preserve near Hutchins Pond. They were also building a cabin on nearby Peabody Mountain, in a spot overlooking the White Mountain National Forest in southern Maine.

I tried hitching to Bethel, but no one seemed to want to pick up a guy with a scruffy beard and a huge pack. When a newspaper reporter came by and asked what I was doing, I said I was hiking the Appalachian Trail and had stayed at the Andover Arms. He photographed me with my "Bethel" sign, and the picture appeared in the paper he worked for the following week. At that moment, though, I still had no ride. Finally, after an hour, Hob's brother Jay, who was antique hunting with a friend, picked me up and dropped me off at a country store where I telephoned my folks, who were staying at Larry and Mary's mountain retreat for the day. My sister Sharon, niece Abbe, Sondra, and Larry's children Evan and Haley

Hob and Deb (The Tandem Teachers) and Jeff (The Lummox) descending Saddleback Mountain after a magnificent day above timberline.

Maine

The Appalachian Trail meanders through
the forest near Little Swift River Pond.

Sunrise on Mt. Abraham in Maine. Mt. Abraham is a 1.6-mile side trail off the Appalachian
Trail. I left Spaulding Mountain Lean-to at 4 a.m. in order to pray and seek God on the Mt.
Abraham summit.

Praising God near the summit of Bemis Mountain.

Nearing the summit of Saddleback Junior.

Mahoosuc Notch in the Mahoosuc Range is a mile-long valley full of huge boulders. In a number of places, I needed to remove my pack and crawl through crevices between rocks. Ice can be found at the bottom of the notch through most of the summer.

An outhouse at Sabbath Day Pond Lean-to, ME. No matter how old such outdoor facilities were, they were always a welcome sight and were more comfortable than using the woods.

were all waiting to see me. We had a wonderful dinner and swim in the pond. Then Larry, Evan and I hiked a mile up Peabody Mountain, where we saw the just-poured cabin foundation. It was a magnificent place.

Rock Piles and Rain

"I scrambled over some boulders, squeezed around others and in places had to remove my pack and crawl through caves created by the in-filling of rock."

I t was sad to say good-bye to Larry and Mary after they drove me and my pack to Grafton Notch. When I began the four-mile ascent of Old Speck (4,180 feet), it was already mid-morning. I had no idea if I would ever see Hob, Deb or Jeff again on my journey. The weather was warm and beautiful as I started off, and after reaching the summit I came down into the Speck Pond Shelter area, which was filled with tent platforms and hikers. This lovely alpine setting contains the highest pond in Maine and is managed by the Appalachian Mountain Club, which charges hikers a fee for staying there. The traffic is so heavy in this area that a full time ranger is assigned to keep things clean and in order.

I continued south over Mahoosuc Arm, descending steeply into one of the most famous parts of the Appalachian Trail, Mahoosuc Notch. Hikers who go through this notch remember it. Many years ago huge boulders fell and piled up on the floor of a mile-long passage between the sheer walls of Mahoosuc Arm Mountain and Fulling Mill Mountain, leaving the way clogged and nearly impassable in places. Following arrows through a labyrinth of small openings between the jagged rocks, I scrambled over some boulders, squeezed around others and in places had to remove my pack and crawl through caves created by the in-filling of rock. Though it was August, I saw ice in some of these places. It took me more than an hour to make it through the notch, and when I came out at its southern end, I was whistling and singing praises.

Then came a flat forested area before the trail went steeply up Fulling Mill Mountain. There I heard people talking and to my surprise found Hob, Deb, Jeff and another southbound thru-hiker, a man from Florida who called himself Swamp Angel. It was great to see everybody again. That night it rained on our camp, but that did not dampen our spirits or story-telling. Awakening later in the darkness, I saw a mouse crawling on my tent's mosquito netting. I flicked the little guy off and went back to sleep.

We began the hike up Fulling Mill Mountain the next morning in rain, and when we reached the summit, the weather grew worse. So without tarrying we headed for Full Goose Shelter – down the sag between Fulling Mill Mountain and South Peak. Ahead of us were four peaks we had to climb before coming to the next shelter. As we reached the summit of Goose Eye's North Peak, at 3,680 feet, the winds picked up to 40 or 50 m.p.h., and in places above timberline, we needed to lean against rocks for balance. We climbed the steep East Peak and then the highest point, the 3,854-foot West Peak of Goose Eye Mountain. Rain came down so hard that in most places the trail was a flowing stream. My soaked boots felt as if they weighed 10 pounds each. At one point on East Peak,

Maine

I almost fell off a 20-foot ledge because of its steepness and the wind. While on the ridge of Goose Eye Mountain we came across a northbound hiker named Footloose, who was being paralleled in his journey by his wife Fancy Free. (She was traveling the Appalachian Trail by road.) In that weather we could not believe that all Footloose was wearing on his upper body was a T-shirt. He said he liked it that way.

After climbing over our last exposed peak, Mt. Carlos, we quickly descended and took the long side trail to Carlos Col Shelter, a structure that is more enclosed than most and has two decks. As we stumbled in, cold and soaked to the bone, the wind was howling through the col and rain was coming down in torrents. And what a crowd there was! On the top deck were nine girls from Camp Aloha, and on the floor below lay a northbound hiker, Jimmy B, from Houston. Next to him there was just enough room for the four of us. With wind-driven rain pelting the shelter, Jimmy B sang "Amazing Grace." Inwardly we all felt safe and warm.

In the morning the wind and rain were just as furious. Although Hob, Deb and I decided to stay another day, Jeff pressed on. The Camp Aloha girls left the shelter late in the morning. Not continuing their hike, they took the side trail down to a road leading into Berlin, New Hampshire. Jimmy B also elected to spend another night at the shelter, so we moved our stuff to the top deck to wait out the storm and enjoy one another's company. The four of us greeted hikers who came in that day, and we were glad to have protection from the storm. In the middle of the afternoon, 13 people in two hiking groups arrived. They were good company, and all night while the storm raged we rested well.

These soggy old wooden puncheons near Cascade Mountain were so slippery that I fell off one and went over my knee in mud.

Carlos Col Shelter was overfilled for two nights due to torrential rain and high winds.

51

Sunrise on the Kennebago River near Rangely, ME.

After canoeing for more than an hour in the fog, we came upon a cow moose and her baby feeding along the river's edge.

This beautiful pond is near the Carter Notch Hut.

Across New England's Highest Peaks

New Hampshire

After saying our good-byes, all 17 of us left Carlos Col Shelter early the next morning. It was an extremely hard 10 miles to the Trident Col Campsite. The trail up and down 3,565-foot Mt. Success was a swift-flowing river like none I had ever seen form on a trail. Compared to those in the area of beautiful Gentian Pond Shelter, the bogs and bog bridges were in horrible shape. Most of the puncheons were old and slippery anyway, and now, with the torrential rain of the last few days, some were floating. A few sank more than a foot into the water when any weight was put on them. I felt like an acrobat crossing a tightrope with my 60-pound pack and heavy wet boots. And indeed I slipped off logs a number of times, sinking over my knee into thick muck – a muddy mixture that was almost like quicksand. One time my foot stuck so hard and fast in it that with all my strength I could hardly pull it free.

Although the hiking was slow and the terrain boggy, the smells of the forest were fragrant and enticing after the heavy rains. My nostrils were filled with a sweet smelling aroma, and the new life that permeated the forest floor seemed to flow around me, giving me renewed energy and strength as I continued south into New Hampshire. Water flowed everywhere on the ridges, in every sag and low place along the trail. Some areas became little ponds that I had to ford in my boots, which were drenched. When I arrived at the Trident campsite, I met a group from Camp Kingswood who were having trouble with their stove, so I lent them mine for the night. The sky had finally begun to clear, providing a beautiful

New wooden puncheons traverse the boggy sections on the Carter-Moriah Trail in the Carter Range, NH.

Climbing over Mt. Hight (4,690 feet) on a cold rainy day in August in the Carter-Moriah Mountain Range, NH

Ascending Mt. Madison with five friends in the Presidential Mountain Range of the White Mountain National Forest, NH.

"God's presence seemed to settle across the mountain tops in the dense fog all day long."

night under the stars. The journey through Maine had taken a month, and I had hiked 275 miles through many valleys and mountain ranges, appreciating the vast unspoiled wilderness. *"What lies ahead I know will be of equal beauty, but now I must concentrate on one day at a time and on each step along the way."*

When Hob, Deb and I woke the following morning, a pungent odor permeated the air. The winds had blown strong sulfur fumes up from a large pulp mill in Berlin, New Hampshire, and we could not believe how strong the rotten egg smell was at 2,000 feet in elevation. As I looked at the map, I found that we were only two and a half miles, as the eagle flies, from the mill, so we quickly packed up and headed over Cascade Mountain and Mt. Hayes. As we ascended Mt. Hayes, we met about a dozen northbound thru-hikers. I had been keeping a count of northbounders I met along the trail, and these hikers brought the list to more than 40. I asked them all how they enjoyed their hikes and what their impressions were. Interestingly, most I met in Maine could not wait until they reached Mt. Katahdin, for their journeys would then be completed. Also, they seemed to be traveling at a faster pace than thru-hikers I met later. Those we met that day seemed to be enjoying their journeys and taking their time. As I moved farther south in my journey, it was good to see the attitude of northbounders change. Many gave me encouragement and shared trail wisdom.

Kinsman on the Trail

We hiked the seven miles down to Route 2, and this took us into Gorham, our next trail town. The nice lady who picked us up on the highway dropped us off at the Gorham House Inn, where we stayed in a place called "The Barn." Jeff and the Swamp Angel had arrived the day before and would be leaving the next morning to climb Mt. Washington. That afternoon I took a long shower, went to a laundromat and visited the post office. Sondra's mother, who knows how much I love onions, had sent me three huge red ones weighing about three pounds. My friends thought I was crazy to put them in my pack. That night we feasted on pizza and salad. My greatest treat to eat when I got into a trail town was salad. Its taste was wonderful, and I felt my body was lacking certain vitamins and minerals that come from salad vegetables.

Very early the next day Ron, the innkeeper, took me to the trail head for the Carter-Moriah Mountain Range. Through the grapevine I had heard that a Chassidic Jew named Rueven was hiking the trail. Northbounders had mentioned him, saying he would travel late at night and come into a shelter and pray out loud. I knew he was in the area because I had seen his gear in The Barn in Gorham. After walking only half a mile down the trail in the early

morning light, I saw a full-bearded man resting on the side of the trail. He was wearing long black pants and a white shirt, and water bottles were sticking out of his pockets. Also, there was a yarmulke on his head, so I knew this must be the famous Rueven.

I introduced myself, and we chatted. Rueven had left New York because he was being threatened by a group of Chassidic men who wanted to force him to grant his wife a divorce. In the Jewish tradition a married man must sign a certificate called a Get in order for a divorce to proceed. When a financial reward was offered to any person who could induce Rueven to sign, he headed for the Appalachian Trail at the suggestion of a friend and had hiked from New York to this point in New Hampshire. I told him of my intention to celebrate the Sabbath on the trail, and he said he believed that was important – adding that he did it himself every Saturday. By 7 a.m. I said good-bye to Rueven and began my five-mile ascent of 4,049-foot Mt. Moriah.

Having left some of my sleeping gear and extra food at The Barn, I planned to hike the Carter-Moriah range in one day with a 25-pound pack. To cover this 20-mile section of the trail, Rueven had hiked all night without a flashlight and occasionally sleeping at the side of the trail. There are 11 peaks over 4,000 feet in this mountain range, the highest being 4,832-foot Carter Dome. The ridges were quite boggy in spots, and many puncheons were placed there to protect the alpine terrain. Drizzle and fog added to the quiet, peaceful atmosphere as I crossed the ridge and went up and down many peaks. God's presence seemed to settle across the mountain tops in the dense fog all day long. I loved photographing the Carter Notch Ponds in this weather, and I stopped by the hut there for a cup of hot chocolate and to read trail registers. The hike down Wildcat Mountain was rocky, steep and very slippery. Sondra and my 10-year old nephew Adam had been waiting to meet me at the Pinkham Notch Lodge since 4 p.m., but I did not finish this difficult section of hiking until two hours later. Even with the lighter pack, this hike was hard on my legs and knees.

We drove back to The Barn to get all my gear, and to my surprise Rueven was still there. He informed me that he was going to be my hiking partner and wanted to ride with me to Jackson, where I would be spending the night. I let him know that my friends in Jackson would not be prepared for him, so he would have to stay at The Barn that night. The idea of a full-time trail experience held no interest for Rueven, so he decided to head south and follow The Peacewalker by hitching rides on country roads. For this reason he said his trail name would be Roadwalker. He indicated that in this manner – by getting on and off the trail – he would parallel my journey, trying to predict the shelters I would be at for various Sabbaths so we might be together.

Rueven began to prepare for the coming Sabbath in a most unusual way. Hikers staying in The Barn that night could not believe their eyes. On an old desk at the top of the stairs, Rueven placed seven candles in a semicircle. As a tablecloth in front of the candles, he spread out a white button-down shirt, and since he could not open anything – because that would denote work, and work is forbidden on the Sabbath – he took the lids off five cans of tuna and three cans of salmon and placed them in a line in front of the candles. Then he put 12 loaves of pita bread next to each other in front of the opened cans. To the right side of all this he set an open bottle of wine and three plastic bottles containing mayonnaise, mustard and ketchup (which he would mix with the fish), along with three bottles of water he would drink from and use for ritual washing of his hands before meals. All this he did before Sabbath observances began. Then, at the right time, Rueven lit the candles, took his prayer book in hand and began to pray and sing his Sabbath melodies. He had donned a long black coat and wrapped a white prayer shawl over his capped head. As he chanted, he rocked back and forth near the table, the candles casting an amber glow around his swaying figure.

Sondra and Adam helped me get my belongings together, and we said farewell to Rueven. I thought I would probably see him farther down the trail. We had dinner with Hob and Deb and then left for Jackson, where we stayed with our friends, Leo and Bobbie, who own a mountain house overlooking the Mt. Washington Valley. *"I had a great day off in Jackson. The rivers were swollen over their banks from the heavy rain last night, and some roads were washed out. We went to the Eastern Mountain Sports store in Conway for some hiking gear, then had a super time eating and talking together."*

The White Mountains

By 1:30 p.m. the next day, five friends from home who came to hike the White Mountains with me had gathered at Pinkham Notch, and we began our journey to the Osgood Tent Sites, which were four miles up the trail. Andrew, Ben and Jeremy had hiked with me in the past, and Steve (The Great White Bowana) and his friend Gary wanted to be along for the next 50 miles of my trek. We all weighed our packs at the Pinkham Notch Lodge, and I found mine to be a heavy 75 pounds. So I went through it again and took out non-essentials, mostly food. Sondra and Adam hiked with us two miles until the trail crossed the Mount Washington Auto Road, then returned to Pinkham Notch. In the late afternoon the rest of us reached the tent sites at the base of Mount Madison and chatted with a northbounder named Featherhead, who was encamped on one of the platforms. It was a beautiful day, and I saw that God had blessed me with wonderful friends to travel with on the trail.

With its elevation gain of 3,000 feet, the two-mile ascent from the campsite to the 5,363-foot summit of Mt. Madison was difficult for me as well as for my friends. Winded and tired, we climbed down to Madison Springs Hut and had lunch. Although the day began with lovely weather, as we walked the highest ridge in New Hampshire, clouds began to flow in and surround the mountain tops. The Gulfside Trail, which is part of the Appalachian Trail, follows the ridge along the Presidential Range of the White Mountains and was all exposed rock for the next seven miles. More than 130 people have lost their lives in climbing Mount Washington – which at 6,288 feet is the highest mountain in the Northeast – and most of them died from exposure to the elements. Some of the world's worst weather, with wind gusts up to 231 m.p.h., has been recorded on the summit. Also, the first cog railway in the world was built on this mountain in 1869, followed by the first weather observatory the next year.

Trail junction near Lonesome Lake, Franconia Notch State Park.

By the time we reached the top, the weather had turned raw – very windy and cold. Jeremy was shivering uncontrollably as we rested in the summit house before descending one mile to the Lake in the Clouds Hut, where I decided to work to pay for my room and board. My friends bunked in a small room under the hut called "The Dungeon," and we ate dinner and breakfast together in the hut. This facility, the largest hut on the trail, can house 90 guests in addition to its staff. We were glad to be there because a raging storm rolled through all night long. After breakfast many guests were trapped inside the hut, and some who tried to climb to the summit to get to their cars or take the van down the auto road were forced back by rain driven by 60 m.p.h. winds.

Steve brought a kite with him to fly in the strong winds above timberline in the Presidential Range.

I had to work in the kitchen until about 9:30 the next morning, so we left at mid-morning, hoping the winds would abate, but they did not. We leaned into heavy side winds as we walked. In the next two hours I stumbled many times as mighty gusts nearly flung me across the exposed ridge. At last, after coming down near Mt. Eisenhower, we got below timberline. Then we climbed 4,310-foot Mt. Pierce before descending to Mizpah Spring Hut, where for $2 we had an all-you-can-eat lentil soup lunch. That filled and warmed us on a bone-chilling day.

We then headed over the last two mountains in the Presidential traverse, 4,052-foot Mt. Jackson and 3,901-foot Mt. Webster. Some bogs along the way were soft and full of water, and using my hiking staff, I tried to measure how far I would sink in if I accidentally fell. Once I was able to push the staff almost completely into the slimy alpine bog. (I thank God for those who built the puncheons, which not only help hikers but also protect fragile ecosystems that take hundreds of years to develop.) From the summit of Mt. Webster, we descended Webster Cliffs into Crawford Notch and came to the Saco River. Because we did not have the

After hiking out of Pinkham Notch, Sondra, my nephew Adam, Steve, Andy, Ben, Gary and Jeremy take a break on the Mt. Washington Auto Road.

The Appalachian Trail near the summit of South Twin Mountain (4,926 feet).

New Hampshire

Beautiful view of Mt. Lafayette and the Franconia Range from Lonesome Lake, NH.

strength to hike to the next shelter, we camped near the river and took a refreshing swim in its swift, cold current. All night long we could hear the river roaring. If I listened closely enough, it seemed as though the churning water was talking to me in a tumult of voices.

The next day we hiked through Crawford Notch and up to Ethan Pond Shelter. By the beautiful pond I lunched on peanut butter and jelly, bagels and gorp (a mixture of M&Ms, raisins and nuts). We decided to continue down the trail in a section that turned out to be the most relaxing three and a half miles so far in my trek. The trail sat on an old railroad bed that gently followed North Fork Brook to Zealand Notch. It seemed to be the first time I could walk and talk and not have to look down at my feet all the time to see if I was going to trip over roots or rocks. I could not believe it – almost four miles of flat hiking. What a joy! We found a campsite before we got to Zealand Falls Hut and took a cold swim in Whitewall Brook. Steve and I had a time of prayer by the water's edge. He and Gary were planning to leave the trail because after the 30 miles of hiking the blisters on their feet had become too painful for them to continue.

The next morning the rest of us climbed Zealand Mountain and then Mt. Guyot at 4,560 feet. On the way we met six northbound hikers – Incline, Doc, Son in Face, Moon in Face, Captain Kook and Hunter. We then climbed over the top of South Twin Mountain at 4,902 feet and descended steeply to Gale Head Hut, where we ate lunch. Situated in the middle of the White Mountain National Forest, this hut is one of the most isolated on the trail. Sitting on the porch afforded us panoramic views of the mountains, without a sound of manmade machinery to be heard. God's peace and presence were everywhere in this mountain paradise. We left the hut and hiked two and a half miles to the Garfield Ridge Campsite, which is half way up Mt. Garfield. The spring, located near the side trail to the campsite, had some of the coldest and best water I ever tasted. That night, as I sat on my tent platform looking up at the myriad of stars twinkling in the heavens, I was filled with God's sweet presence and overjoyed at being in the midst of a mountain wilderness.

I was eager to write in my journal. *"God's Word has been a lamp unto my feet and a light unto my path. I will seek His kingdom and righteousness first and learn to judge rightly. Sometimes, like the present moment, God's words fill me to the point where I have to share them with others or enter them in my journal. It is a privilege to walk with God in the wilderness and experience all the beauty of His magnificent creation. At times, His peace and presence are so overwhelming that I want to shout out praises to Him. In so many of these beautiful places I could remain for weeks if I had the time. I am thankful that I do not have to rush to complete this journey. I want to seek God's timing and walk in His steps, all the way down to Georgia."*

New Hampshire

Bump in the Night

Ben, Andrew, Jeremy and I left the campsite early on a cool, crisp morning and ascended to the rocky summit of Mt. Garfield at 4,488 feet. The Franconia Ridge lay ahead of us, and we came down Garfield only to begin a steep two-mile ascent of 5,249-foot Mt. Lafayette, the highest mountain in the Franconia range. Standing atop this summit gave us views of the entire western White Mountain region. Fortunately, the weather was perfect for our four-mile hike along the jagged, exposed Franconia Ridge, which crosses Mt. Lincoln at 5,089 feet and Little Haystack Mountain at 4,760 feet. From the ridge we followed the trail down to Liberty Spring Campsite and tasted the best spring water in the White Mountains.

We decided not to stay and to hike farther down the mountain and camp closer to Franconia Notch since the boys would be picked up there the following morning. Two miles down the trail we stopped for a rest and a drink from a brook. We had been looking for a campsite because we did not want to camp in the busy area of Franconia Notch. While I was sitting by the brook, I suddenly heard my name being called. Then I heard it again. Knowing all the boys were downstream getting a drink, I thought this was strange, so I climbed up the embankment and to my surprise saw a beautiful campsite in the woods that no one could see from the trail. I could not believe my eyes and began to thank God for His goodness in providing a perfect place to stay for the night. The boys could not believe it either when they saw the place, which was just large enough for our two tents.

By carefully putting leaves and sticks over the site when we departed the following morning, we left no trace of our presence. As we climbed down to Franconia Notch, we saw a hiker walking quickly up the trail. It happened to be Dan Bruce (trail name Wingfoot), who had hiked the trail many times and was the author of a valuable resource called *The Thru-hiker's Handbook*. Dan was trying intently to complete still another thru-hike, but he stopped to talk for a while and was very friendly. After traveling down the trail another mile, we crossed the Pemigewasset River and walked to "The Flume," where the boys called for their ride home. I felt sad in seeing them off but thankful for the fellowship we had on the trail.

I hiked the three miles from there up to Lonesome Lake Hut and decided to work for my last stay in a hut. The crew made me work so much that I could not wait to leave the place. In the afternoon they assigned me the task of taking all the garbage that had piled up under the hut, which seemed like a ton, and burn it a hundred yards away near a putrid compost pile. Then I enjoyed a glorious swim in the lake, with fantastic views of the Franconia Ridge reflecting in the water. I washed dishes for three more hours until

Crossing the Pemigewasset River in Franconia Notch, NH.

I finally got to eat dinner, which was delicious. In the hut that night I met Leon Backman, the 38th person to thru-hike the Appalachian Trail. It was great talking with him and hearing how the trail has changed over time.

That night, as I slept soundly in a top bunk in one of the rooms, I was suddenly awakened by a tremendous thud and then a frightening scream. I knew exactly what had happened. A sleeping child had fallen from one of the highest bunks onto the wooden floor. Many people including me ran with flashlights to where the boy was lying and saw that he was bleeding from his mouth. We carried him to the dining hall and determined that, fortunately, he had received only a swollen lip from his six-foot fall. I will never forget the sound of that thud and the piercing scream that followed it.

I wanted to get going very early the next morning, so I asked the crew if I could leave before breakfast – knowing that if I ate breakfast there, I would be beholden to work for it, and it might be noon before I got on my way again. The trail led up to Kinsman Pond Shelter, where I found Rueven waiting for me to celebrate the Sabbath. He had tried to predict where I would be this time and said he would try again for the next Sabbath. I left him as he was, praying in front of Kinsman Shelter in the early morning mist. Wearing his black fur cap and white prayer shawl, he was moving rhythmically back and forth to the chanting of his prayers.

The trail steeply ascended North Kinsman and then crossed over to South Kinsman at 4,358 feet. The descent from South Kinsman, one of the steepest on the trail, could be very dangerous when wet. While I was climbing down a particularly steep section, a legend came to life before my eyes. I had heard about a northbound thru-hiker whose trail name was Geek and Ziggy. Supposedly, Geek had picked up a kitten on a canoe trip before he started hiking the trail, and he let the kitten hike along with him at the beginning of his journey in Georgia. The kitten did not hike fast, nor did it like the rain, so Geek would put it in or on top of his pack, or so it was said. There on South Kinsman I met Geek hiking, and sure enough, Ziggy was on top of his pack – although the animal did not look like a kitten anymore. Ziggy now weighed more than 10 pounds, and Geek acknowledged that food he carried for him added to the weight of his pack.

I went on to Eliza Brook Shelter, then up and over Mt. Wolf at 3,478 feet, where I met Recline and Good Vibes. Later that afternoon, exhausted after 13 and a half miles of hiking, I came into Beaver Brook Shelter. That night in the shelter I met northbounders named The Volunteer, Joe, Pathfinder and The Nylon Machine. While walking the ridge on Mt. Wolf, my senses were so filled with God's peace and the glory of the natural surroundings that I had to stop and write in my journal.

While descending South Kinsman Peak, I met a northbound thru-hiker named Geek and Ziggy. Geek had found a kitten before hiking the Appalachian Trail and carried him on his pack from Georgia to Maine.

New Hampshire

"while I was climbing down a particularly steep section, a legend came to life before my eyes."

"What does it mean to be a Peacewalker? To see and appreciate every step I take; to be aware of each breath; to smell the fragrance in the air; to touch the ferns and pines that surrounded me; to see God glorified in all His creation; to look around me and appreciate the life with which God has blessed me; to hear the stillness of nature; to feel the breeze pouring over my body, listening as it rustles through the trees; to gaze on cascading waterfalls and see life ever flowing from God's eternal plan. Quiet stillness, stir my soul to seek God and hear the Master's voice when He calls. Let me feel the presence of His Spirit as the breezes flow past me and through the trees. Help me see you, O God, in the sunlight of your love. Warm my heart and melt it to purify me and make me holy. Keep my feet on the right path and upon the solid foundation of your Word. Please don't let them slip, but help me walk with You in peace."

Airborne

The hike to Mt. Moosilauke is one of the best in the White Mountains. The steep ascent follows a magnificent waterfall for three quarters of a mile and then, after another two and a half miles, comes to a 4,802-foot summit. For a hiker going south, the mountain is the last whose top is above timber-line, and from that point – a heavenly spot on this beautifully clear day – I could see into five states. I then descended the six miles to Glencliff, my next trail town. A friendly man named Hank, whose house was near the post office, had put soft drinks on his porch for hikers to purchase on an honor system. I gladly bought two refreshing sodas and went to pick up my mail.

After gathering my new supplies and sending unwanted items home, I called Roger Brickner, who has hosted thousands of thru-hikers in homes in both New York and New Hampshire. Roger now lived in an early-1800s federal style house on a scenic common near Glencliff. He would come for hikers at the post office, take them to his home, feed them a hearty dinner, let them sleep in his barn, and then, after a hearty breakfast in the morning, return them to the trail. I called between 3 and 4 p.m., and within 15 minutes Roger's friend Sven picked me up and drove me to the beautiful home. After touring Roger's mini-weather station and viewing a beautiful 36-foot Appalachian Trail mural, I cleaned up for supper. We feasted on spaghetti and talked about everything. Roger, who taught history in New York schools for 30 years, was now enjoying his hobby as a weather watcher in addition to traveling and entertaining hikers.

Dropped off at the trail early the next morning, I began one of my longest hiking days – 19 miles with a full pack. After climbing Mt. Mist and Mt. Cube at 2,911 feet, I met a northbounder named Dead Ahead, who hiked with a dog and was listening to the Grateful Dead on his Walkman. When I arrived at Hexacuba Shelter on the side of Mt. Cube (one of the newer shelters on the trail), I found a northbound hiker named John the Baptist lying sick and asleep in his sleeping bag. The Dartmouth Outing Club, which takes care of this part of the trail, designed and built the six-sided structure along with a five-sided outhouse nearby, called the Pentaprivy. I was happily hiking down the trail on Mt. Cube, singing as I went, when I suddenly slipped on a wet log, did a complete flip in the air with my 65-pound pack and landed flat on my back. Stunned for a second, I looked at the tree tops and blue sky, then continued singing where I left off, hardly skipping a beat. It must have been quite a scene for any animals watching me.

Dartmouth and Dinner

After descending Mt. Cube to Jacobs Brook, I began my ascent of Smarts Mountain. On the way I met Noreen, The Psych Hiker, and to my surprise caught up with Hob and Deb, who were close to finishing their Appalachian Trail journey. Along with another thru-hiker, Banjo, we had a great little reunion on the 3,240-foot summit of Smarts Mountain. It was August 21, and I celebrated my 34th birthday on that summit as well, thanking God for the strength He had given me to reach this point in my journey. Before leaving the summit I visited the pit toilet there. This was like sitting in an automobile because a pedal, steering wheel and other car paraphernalia had been built into the facility.

Hob, Deb and I then hiked over many steep ledges on our way over Moose Mountain. We were so exhausted after hiking more than 15 miles that we knew we were not going to make it to Velvet Rocks Shelter, so we camped by a small stream. Having met eight northbounders that day, I saw that my total was more than 90. After a fair night's sleep we got up early and meandered over fairly flat trails, traveling through beautiful pastures, fields and pine forests, up rocky ledges, across sludgy beaver ponds and finally into the town of Hanover, the home of Dartmouth College. The trail went through the center of town and by the campus. Hob and Deb ended their complete hike of the Appalachian Trail on the common, and we looked forward to a great dinner to celebrate.

Fortunately, for there is no inexpensive housing in Hanover, a number of Dartmouth fraternities allow hikers to sleep on their premises. We tried to find a good, quiet fraternity to stay in, but the three we went to would have been either noisy or smoky. While wandering around town, we met another thru-hiker, Mr. Bill, and had dinner with him in an eating spot famous with hikers, Everything But Anchovies – with its all-you-can-eat pasta specials. After dinner Hob, Deb and I hiked back up the trail past the soccer field on the edge of town and camped in the woods. That was a much better way for Hob and Deb to spend their last night on the Appalachian Trail.

New Hampshire

In the morning I said good-bye to The Tandem Teachers and waited for my father and Sondra to pick me up. I had to go home for a few days because I was going to be in the wedding party of one of my best friends, Mike, who had traveled cross-country with me after we graduated from college. During the few days I spent at home, all I could think about was getting back into the wilderness and onto the trail again. I had to visit an outdoor equipment store, REI, to exchange my boots for a new pair because my old ones had begun to break apart in many places and the soles were coming off. In taking care of this, I realized the unfortunate fact that until the new boots were broken in, blisters would begin to form again. The wedding went great, and I also visited my 100-year old Grandpa Joe. The following day I packed for Vermont.

Appalachian Trail sign next to Lonesome Lake Hut, White Mountain National Forest, NH.

Patches of sulphur mushrooms grow on decaying trees and in the moist soil of the Green Mountains.

Lush Forests of the Green Mountains

Vermont

After being dropped off in the center of Hanover, I crossed over the Connecticut River and headed into Norwich, Vermont. The trail followed roads toward the town and then turned off into woods leading up to Griggs Mountain. My feet, beginning the tortuous process of breaking in new boots, felt as painful as they did in the 100-Mile Wilderness. I was glad I kept my sneakers with me because four miles outside of Hanover I could not continue in the boots. As I neared Happy Hill Shelter, the oldest shelter on the trail, I saw a fast-paced red-haired hiker with a light pack traveling towards me. In an instant I knew, although I had never met him, that this was the famous Ward Leonard, who had hiked the Appalachian Trail many times and held the speed record for it. As Ward strode by me at his three- to four-mile an hour pace, I said, "Hi there" and got no response – hardly a look. I had heard that this could at times be Ward's trail manner. I would have enjoyed talking with him, but he seemed to have no time for an overburdened hiker like me.

I continued in my sneakers toward the White River and West Hartford, stopping to buy vegetables at an organic farm along the road walk. The trail quickly entered the woods after crossing the river, and I tried to make it to Cloudland Shelter by dark. My body and feet ached so that I had to camp by a beautiful brook along the trail, three miles from the shelter, where I had a delicious dinner with vegetables I had purchased from the farm. The trail through Vermont had been relocated in many places during the past few years to take it off roads and up into the mountains. The

The foliage along the trail was magnificent. This hobblebush was bursting with summer berries.

many relocations led the trail over beautiful meadows, through pastures with cows, near farms, and across very hilly terrain. I barely made the 13 miles to the red-roofed Winturi Shelter by dusk. My feet hurt from new blisters beginning to form in the usual places. I spent the night with The Connecticut Yankee in the shelter. Thru-hikers I had seen that day included The Posse, Indiana Dan, Aqua Slug, Dobie Ma, Ramblin' Dan, AB Positive and Lone Star. I also saw Rueven, who was staying at an old shelter off the trail and wondering where I would be for the next Sabbath. I told him I had no idea because I never really knew where I would be at the end of any day on the trail. The next morning I climbed a ridge to a fire tower called The Lookout. The trail followed scenic old logging roads in this area, where I met Moose on the Loose and Spike the Hike. I continued down the wooded trail to Stony Brook Shelter, where I met a man named John and his son Lucas. The three of us climbed a dry section of trail on a new relocation over Quimby Mountain.

Blind Faith

I made a quick seven-mile trek across the Vermont mountainside to Mountain Meadows Lodge. Sondra was going to meet me there but had not arrived, and no other hikers were staying there. I was able to work in the kitchen for my dinner, cleaning a lot of pots, pans and dishes. I also met a newspaper reporter who wanted to talk to me about the trail. He was anticipating an interview with a famous northbound thru-hiker, Bill Irwin, who was hiking the whole Appalachian Trail with his seeing-eye dog Orient. Everyone on the trail had heard of Bill's courageous journey. Reporters were meeting him everywhere. I had heard that Bill was a Christian who felt that God prompted him to hike the trail even though he was blind. In that I believed God also spoke to me about hiking this trail, it was going to be a privilege to meet Bill. That night I prayed that God would give Bill strength to finish the hike and protect him and Orient along the way. In the morning Dennis, the reporter, began hiking with me up the long ridge that led to Mt. Killington. After we covered a few miles, we came to Maine Junction, where the Appalachian Trail joins the Long Trail, our country's first long distance trail (completed in 1931). The Long Trail crosses Vermont from the Canadian to the Massachusetts border, a distance of 265 miles – of which a 100-mile section on the southern end is now the Appalachian Trail as well.

When we got up to Pico Camp shelter, another four miles up the trail, we met Sondra, The Walking Dude and Jeremiah. After eating some lunch we proceeded up to Cooper Lodge near the summit of Mt. Killington, which, at 4,235 feet, is the second highest mountain in Vermont. Along this section of trail, we met Bill Irwin and Orient coming from the opposite direction. Bill's trail

...nt. Killington is a stone shelter built in 1939.

Rueven has just about taken over Cooper Lodge with all his provisions for the Sabbath.

name was The Orient Express because he felt that he was like a train being pulled by his wonderful dog. To my surprise, Bill was hiking not only with other northbounders but also with Rueven. I do not know how Rueven knew where I would be on the trail, but there he was with Bill and Orient. Rueven had been staying at Cooper Lodge and decided to walk with Bill on the trail for a while. I had a great time talking with Bill, and he took my address so my name could be added to his newsletter address list. In this way I would hear more about his journey. I wrote in my journal that day. *"It was great meeting this man of faith. I have prayed for his eyes to see and strength for each day of his journey. May he be a light for the Lord to all he meets, and may good friends always be a blessing to him."*

Sondra, Rueven and I then hiked towards Cooper Lodge, where we would be spending the night. Rueven spent hours getting ready for the Sabbath. Using a small wood burning stove and a large candle, he made a slow-cooked meal called "cholent," but it did not turn out well. He then spent three hours fervently praying into the night. It was a cold, damp and uncomfortable night, for the large stone shelter was occupied by a dozen or so mice that traveled about us like a small army looking for food. For some reason Rueven got up at 5:30 in the morning to pray again – loudly, I may add – and woke us up. I asked him to pray softly until it was time for the rest of us to get up.

Later that morning we all took the short side trail up to the summit of Mt. Killington. Rueven was in his full Sabbath regalia, his body wrapped in his large white prayer shawl. He also wore a long black coat, and on his head was a round, wide-rimmed fur hat. As we neared the peak, Rueven began chanting a Sabbath melody for all the people who had taken the chair lift up to hear. It was quite a scene. I overheard one girl asking her mother why this man was singing, and the mother's reply was that he must be very happy.

On the summit we were blessed with crisp clear weather – a brilliant sun shining in a rich blue sky – and we could see into five states as well as Canada. Sondra and I returned to the shelter to pack up. I headed south off Mt. Killington while Sondra climbed to the summit to take the chair lift down. The Appalachian Trail travels through dense evergreen forests near the summit and through hardwoods at lower elevations on its way to Governor Clement Shelter, which is in a clearing by Sargent Brook.

On that beautiful summer evening near the end of August, I hiked the six miles to Clarendon Shelter, where I met Sondra, who had hiked in from the south. The shelter was full of campers, including thru-hikers Dreamer and Grasshopper. After talking with our new friends until late in the night, I found my thoughts turning to God in prayer. *"I have come across a section in the book of Exodus that says the Sabbath was to be a sign between God's people and Himself, a day holy to God. There must be something wonderful about this day because even God rested on the seventh day of creation. So I have decided that it will also be special to*

"we could see into five states as well as canada".

The trail in eastern Vermont goes through many hills and a lot of scenic farm land. Dana Hill is a high pasture in which hikers climb over one of hundreds of stiles built along the trail.

This beaver pond near South Adler Brook is one of many in southern Vermont.

me. *Hoping to walk more closely with God, I am committing myself to observe a day of rest each week and not to hike."*

Pack Mishap

"The skies darkened, and deep rumbling could be heard for more than an hour before the tumult finally arrived."

The trail through southern Vermont is well maintained and meanders through beautiful, lush forests. The 15 miles to the Danby-Landgrove Road passed along the scenic White Rocks and then down to a pristine pond called Little Rock. Sondra, utilizing her car, had been hiking in the opposite direction on the trail, and we met at Little Rock Shelter. A huge thunderstorm was coming slowly in from the northwest. The skies darkened, and deep rumbling could be heard for more than an hour before the tumult finally arrived. I thanked God that we were not on the ridge when the wild storm finally struck. There was more lightning, thunder and torrential rain in those 45 minutes than I had ever seen. We kept walking even though the trail had turned into a rushing river. Fortunately, being deep in the forest, we were protected from the lightning raging overhead. Then, as quickly as the storm had come, it ended, and we came out of the wilderness onto muddy Danby Road, soaked. Sondra drove us to Sun Lodge on Bromley Mountain, where I wrote postcards to friends. That night I asked God to travel with me as He did with Moses. *"If only I could remain faithful to Him every day of the journey, here in the wilderness!"*

Having been on the trail almost two months, I was getting into shape – able to hike 17 miles without feeling too much pain. In the morning I began hiking from the Danby Road where the trail climbs past Lost Pond Shelter to the summit of Baker Peak. There, amid grand views of southern Vermont, I met a northbounder, Mr. Moleskin, who was hiking with his nephew. After talking for a while, we exchanged addresses in order to share photos when our journeys were completed. As the trail descended slightly for two miles, I came to beautiful Griffith Lake, which is surrounded by shelters and tent platforms. As I neared it, the trail turned into a raised boardwalk on which I took a short snack break. I was getting ready to leave when I noticed a couple hiking on the Lake Trail, which intersects the Appalachian Trail right where I was standing. Jeff and Suzie introduced themselves, and after talking a few minutes we realized our common faith in the Lord. This brief fellowship on the trail was sweet, and I promised to visit them in Knoxville when I entered the Smoky Mountains.

The trail continued climbing along the ridge to Peru Peak at 3,429 feet, then over Styles Peak. On top of Bromley Mountain I met Stone Stomper, who said few northbounders were left behind him. The trail went by ski lifts and over ski trails near the summit. Sondra met me there, and we hiked the two and a half miles down to Routes 11 and 30. Then she drove me to the Chalet Motel in

Manchester. I had planned to stay at the Zion Episcopal Church hostel, but it had just closed for the season. In the morning I walked two miles to the post office, where I met two men, Bob and Tom, who invited me to their home for breakfast and gave me a ride back to the motel. After I got packed, I stood by the road looking for a ride back to the trail head, five miles away. Soon Bob, Tom and their wives drove by and graciously offered me a ride. God is truly faithful!

Carrying a full 70 pounds again, I found the next 10 miles strenuous. Three miles up the trail I came to Spruce Peak Shelter, with its double bunks, wood burning stove, sliding door and an ice cold spring. I felt I should go on but resolved to return to this beautiful spot some day. Continuing through the forest, I reached secluded Stratton Pond, took a refreshing swim, then walked around to Bigelow Shelter. It was September, and the weather was cooler, especially at night. Also, the trail was becoming less crowded because most children had returned to school. I spent the night with Ray, a Manchester chiropractor, and his dog, Melissa. Ray was planning, as I was, to hike over Stratton Mountain the next day, so in the morning we took the three-mile ascent together and then, in a cool, foggy wind, climbed the fire tower. We came down the mountain on a new trail relocation to Story Spring Shelter. On relocations the walking can be difficult because small, freshly cut tree trunks stick up out of the ground and grab at your feet.

By the time I got to Story Spring, I was tired but decided to go on. Ray parted with me there because he wanted to hike to Goddard Shelter, which was farther than I wanted to go. I took my time photographing beaver ponds and berries and ferns. On the ridge near Kid Gore Shelter, however, I slipped on a mossy rock and fell hard on my pack once again. This time I heard a slight crack as I landed. When I got to the shelter and took off my pack, I saw that the frame was split. This frustrated me beyond words because a frame in two pieces makes a fully loaded pack almost unusable. Fog and clouds filled the shelter all that night. In the morning Just Al, who also camped in the shelter, helped me fix the frame by squeezing cuttings from a sapling into the frame tubing and tying two saplings to the frame for extra support. To my surprise the pack stood solidly, and I could continue on my journey.

I hiked the four miles over the summit of Glastenbury Mountain at 3,748 feet and climbed the fire tower, where I had lunch. What an awesome view! The four miles up Glastenbury were rough. My boots were still hurting me at times, and blisters were forming on the back of my heels. Even so, I went on to Melville Nauheim Shelter, which was eight miles away. The trail went over Little Pond Mountain and along Porcupine Ridge. When I got to the shelter, I met Carl, who was hiking a portion of the Long Trail and who also loves photography. We took pictures in the morning fog outside the shelter and then hiked south on the

Andy looks over to Mt. Greylock from East Mountain, MA.

Rueven saying his morning prayers at Congdon Camp.

Many thru-hikers, Scouts and families enjoy Clarendon Shelter on a beautiful August evening.

Just Al helped me fix my broken pack at Kid Gore Shelter, Vermont.

Appalachian Trail where it passes through a huge broken boulder called Split Rock.

Sabbath

The two-mile descent to Route 9 was steep and slippery. I needed to call the Kelty company, so I decided to go into Bennington. A man named Benton was sitting in his car in the parking area on the road while I was trying to hitch a ride in heavy drizzle. Seeing that I was unsuccessful, he drove over and offered to take me into town. From a phone booth I spoke to a Kelty representative who said he would immediately ship a frame to my next trail town, which was 30 miles away. The saplings were beginning to bend. I prayed that they would hold. Before hitching the five miles back to the trail, I ate at a local diner. I then walked a mile down the road and set my pack against the first Route 9 signpost I saw. Within two minutes a man named J.J. picked me up. I then hiked four miles in rain and fog to Congdon Camp, pushing to reach the shelter before dark. It was late Friday afternoon, and I was looking forward to my first Sabbath Day rest on the trail.

With each passing day in my walk with God in the wilderness, the idea of resting one day a week had become more intriguing. Ever since I was young and growing up in a wonderful Jewish home, my faith in God had been strong. Yet over the years, and especially after reading the New Testament, my belief in God had expanded. After much careful thought, deliberation and prayer, I came to the conclusion that Jesus – Yeshua in Hebrew – was, and is, the fulfillment of God's perfect plan for all people to come into close relationship with Him. For this reason I am considered quite "different" by many of my Jewish friends, but I try to show my love to them and to everyone as I walk the journey of life each day. Celebrating Sabbath days on the trail, I believed, would bring me to a new level in my walk with God.

When I arrived at the shelter, I was surprised to see Rueven standing outside, making his Sabbath preparations. The Congdon Camp shelter is an enclosed cabin with bunks and a wood burning stove. Rueven and I talked for a bit before I unloaded my gear and cooked a dinner. With the prospect of a full day's rest awaiting me, I had a great night's sleep. Rueven and I talked in the morning, and then he went off to say his prayers. For hours I sat under trees by a nearby stream, praying and seeking God. I thanked the Lord for His goodness to me and enjoyed His presence by the waters. *"My heart is toward you, O Lord. I pray that You will speak to your servant, so I may know Your will and way more fully. Open my mind, my ears and my eyes to see You clearly. I love you, Lord, with all my heart."*

During the day hikers named George, Jim and Andy came

Vermont

into the shelter, intending to spend the night. After dinner Rueven began chanting a Devar Torah, a message about the passage in the Bible he was studying that week. The rest of us were mesmerized as he spoke, chanted and then cried about the blessings and the curses that would fall upon God's children depending on whether they followed Him. It was strangely coincidental that the passage Rueven was reading was chanted at my Bar Mitzvah more than 20 years earlier. Rueven's chanting and crying intensified as he contemplated the destruction of the Holy Temple in Jerusalem nearly 2,000 years ago. In a few hours we all fell asleep, reflecting deeply on a most unusual evening.

Because I had met no southbound thru-hikers since Gorham, New Hampshire, it was great to see Andy – trail name Pig Pen. He had been hiking with friends Rich (Speed) and Brandy (The Beastmaster), who had taken a few days off and would meet him down the trail in Massachusetts. The three had graduated from high school in Cincinnati and started on the trail more than two weeks after I did. In the morning Andy and I said good-bye to Rueven and headed south. After hiking 10 miles over beautiful forested ridges, we came to the Vermont/Massachusetts border. It was hard to imagine that I had hiked more than two months and 580 miles since leaving Mount Katahdin.

It was mid-September, and the forests were beginning to show signs of autumn. In the four miles we walked before descending into North Adams, Massachusetts, we crossed several ledges and met Desperado hiking with his dog, Misty. Desperado had hiked the trail more than once and was doing a small section for just a few weeks. We had a mile of road-walking to cross North Adams before heading up into the woods again. The trail passed by Mt. Williams Reservoir and then became extremely steep. It was the end of a long hiking day, and another storm was racing in. Trying to beat out the rain, Andy went quickly on to Wilbur Clearing Shelter, which is half way up Mt. Greylock. I arrived there about half an hour later, very cold and wet from the pelting rain. Overnight the temperature dropped into the mid-40s, and the wind was gusty. As the storm raged, we slept comfortably in the shelter.

"With each passing day in my walk with God in the wilderness, the idea of resting one day a week had become more intriguing."

Jug End follows the Laconic Range in the Berkshires, with breathtaking views of southern Massachusetts.

Through the Beautiful Berkshires

Massachusetts

Morning brought a brisk north wind with puffy clouds – cool weather that eased the three-mile climb of Mt. Greylock. With a summit of 3,487 feet, Greylock is the highest mountain in Massachusetts and is accessible by car. In Bascom Lodge we met hikers who had just finished northbound thru-hikes and were now working in the lodge. They treated us to huge pieces of cake. Then, as the clouds around the summit broke free, Andy and I began our eight-mile descent, the trail coming out of the forest near our next trail town, Cheshire, Massachusetts. As we came into town, we were greeted by his hiking buddies, Rich and Brandy, who had just come down Mt. Greylock themselves. We all walked to St. Mary's Catholic Church, which allows hikers to stay on its large parish hall floor for free. In this way Father Tom and his congregation have been a blessing to hundreds of hikers each year. Leaving our gear in the hall, we went to the post office – and yes, the new pack frame was waiting for me! The saplings had held for more than 35 miles of rough terrain. After we brought our supplies to the church, Father Tom showed us around. We then washed up, went out for pizza and bought food. When we returned, Father Tom showed us *5 Million Steps*, a video on the Appalachian Trail, while we ate a half gallon of Oreo ice cream. I worked past midnight replacing my old pack frame.

In the morning, after Andy and I went out for breakfast, I loaded my pack. This laborious and frustrating task took me hours, and I did not leave the church until 2 p.m., so I was in a rush to get to the next shelter before dark. The climb up The Cobbles, while

Larry (The Tortoise) was the last northbound thru-hiker I met in the north.

The summit and tower on Mt. Greylock (3,491 feet), the highest mountain in Massachusetts.

Massachusetts

Standing on the footbridge that crosses the Massachusetts Turnpike brought to mind the time when I first began to dream of hiking the entire Appalachian Trail. Traveling by car on the highway below, I pictured myself standing on this very bridge.

Mike, the caretaker of Upper Goose Pond Cabin, heads out in his canoe to get fresh drinking water.

"Near sunset I finally arrived at the place that had first inspired me to take this wonderful journey."

very hard, afforded great views of Cheshire and Mt. Greylock. The next seven miles over the rocky, root-filled ridge to Dalton was long and difficult with my now heavy pack. I reached Dalton exhausted, barely able to walk the three-mile road through town. At one point I sat on a curb for 20 minutes to get enough energy to go on. The one-mile ascent up Grange Hall Road was very tiring, and by the time I reached the place where the Appalachian Trail heads off into the woods, the sun had set. I could not believe I had put myself into such a predicament. I looked into the dark woods and could see only blackness; then I looked up and saw bright stars twinkling in the clear night sky.

Never having hiked after dark, I was apprehensive about entering the woods. I hesitated on the lonesome road for a while, hoping for something to change, then summoned energy and courage, donned my head lamp and stepped into the pitch black forest. It was three-quarters of a mile to Kay Wood Shelter. As I stumbled along, I searched for blazes so I would not get off the trail. At times my mind ran away with thoughts about what might be lurking in the woods. After what seemed like more than an hour, I came to the side trail sign for the shelter and began my descent. Near the shelter I began to worry about what or whom I might find there. With my head lamp I peered around a corner of the beautiful Adirondack-style structure and found it empty. Quickly I unloaded my gear, got out a change of clothes and my water bag and headed to the stream, which was down a steep hill. I felt like a scared animal as I washed and gathered water for dinner. I kept looking around, trying to hear muffled noises in the woods above the din of the rambling stream. Finally, I scrambled back up the embankment, settled comfortably in the shelter and fixed a trail feast: Sloppy Joe mix and noodles. After an exhausting and adventurous day, this dinner was superb.

A Dream Fulfilled

I did not leave the shelter until late morning because I was so tired. Even so, I decided to try to go more than 18 miles to Upper Goose Pond Cabin. The terrain was not too hilly, but in stepping over thousands of roots and rocks and going around many boggy beaver dams, I found the hiking quite strenuous. When I arrived at the newly constructed October Mountain Lean-to, I wanted to stay there (and probably should have), but I pushed on. Near sunset I finally arrived at the place that had first inspired me to take this wonderful journey, the Appalachian Trail's crossing of the Massachusetts Turnpike. Ten years earlier I had dreamed of standing on the footbridge that crossed that highway, and now here I was! It was hard to believe, after all the years of waiting, that I was finally doing this. The moment would have been even more mem-

Massachusetts

orable had I not been pushing myself so hard. I was exhausted, and Upper Goose Pond was still a mile and a half away. I rested on the bridge for a while, thanking God for providing this time in my life to walk with Him in the wilderness. The seed He had planted in my heart a decade earlier had truly grown into fruition.

When I arrived at the cabin at dusk, I was greeted by Mike, the caretaker, and Larry (The Tortoise) from Florida. Larry was the last northbounder I met up north on the trail. I took a refreshing swim in the beautiful glacial pond in front of the cabin, then settled into a bunk. The three of us talked until late in the evening. I awoke from a fitful night's sleep with a slight stomach ache. This was the first time in the journey that I had felt sick. I must have been pushing too hard. My stomach was still sore as I began to hike around the shore of Upper Goose Pond, continuing south along the ridges of the Berkshire Mountains in western Massachusetts. Within five miles I came in sight of another hiker, Jim from Florida, who was on a week's outing. He was also heading south, so we hiked 10 miles together that day, climbing up over Baldy Mountain and then down through a road walk near Tyringham.

On this Indian-summer day, as the trail headed up a dirt road into Beartown State Forest, the mosquitoes came at us in a torrential drove. We could not stop to rest for a second. I had not experienced such a frenzied attack since my days in the 100-Mile Wilderness. *"There were millions of them. It was tortuous."* We finally got off the old country road and headed into the forest to Mt. Wilcox, passing by Mt. Wilcox North Shelter since there was little water there and continuing to Mt. Wilcox South Shelter. I set up my tent in the shelter because the mosquitoes were still looking savagely for a meal, and I needed a good night's rest. Such a large insect population seemed unusual in the middle of September, but for the three previous days we had such warm weather.

Genuine Rest

Jim and I had a leisurely five and a half mile hike to our next stop. The Tom Leonard Shelter, with its two bunks, high loft, picnic tables and a beautiful view across East Mountain State Forest, is one of the nicest shelters on the trail. As I walked the long path down to the stream, I caught sight of a person getting water and could not believe my eyes. It was Rueven! He was filling his half-dozen water bottles to prepare for the Sabbath. After washing in the stream, I gathered water and walked back up to the shelter. We had a relaxing afternoon, and I had a great night's sleep despite the mosquitoes. After midnight a storm came through with heavy rain and lightning. There is nothing like being snug in a sleeping bag and going to sleep to the pleasant sound of rain drumming on the roof of a shelter.

"Today was my second day of rest as I sat on the tent platform, Bible in hand, communing with God. What a gift to experience such peace and God's presence in this quiet wilderness setting! It was still a struggle for me to rest on a beautiful day like this and know the trail was calling me to move on. I am learning to slow down from the fast paced life that has always whirled about me. I need to learn to take the time to stop, listen, and enjoy what I have been blessed with. By taking a day off and resting from the week's work, I am beginning to see each day a little differently. While sitting on the deck and wandering around the shelter area, I noticed the day's coming and going more closely than I ever had. The sun's rising and setting were ingrained into my being as I fully experienced the gentle passing of time. The day's finale was special – the golden sun setting slowly and sending a splash of pastels across the horizon, followed by quiet darkness, like a soft blanket held in strong arms, being wrapped around me and the whole countryside."

An awesome inner peace, like nothing I had ever experienced, settled upon my soul and remained with me through the night. As I sat in stillness for hours that day, my senses were heightened, and I felt enlightened regarding the operation of God's natural order. I saw more clearly and heard more keenly. I prayed that this spiritual insight would flow into my daily life and change me. As a cool breeze drifted into the shelter, taking most of the mosquitoes away, another joyful and pleasant night's sleep overcame me.

The next day would also be relaxing because I had friends visiting me from home. This shelter was one of the closest to my home and to the nearest road. I walked two miles to Route 23 near Great Barrington to meet Sondra and our friends Shoshanah and her two sons, Saul and Eli. They took me to a great breakfast place in Great Barrington, where I spoke on the phone with Shoshanah's son Jesse, one of my former students, who could not make the trip. While we sat at the breakfast table, they gave me the shocking news of a southbound couple named Geoff (Clevis) and Molly (Nalgene) who had been murdered on the trail two days before. After climbing out of Duncannon, Pennsylvania, two other southbounders, Biff and Cindy, had found the bodies of Geoff and Molly in a shelter. No one knew why these two sweet people were killed. Heartbroken, I prayed that the Holy Spirit would comfort their families and friends and all the hikers who knew them. Most other southbounders were about a month ahead of me down the trail from where this incident occurred. Law enforcement officials had posted signs and told hikers they should stay off the trail until the person responsible was apprehended.

After breakfast the five of us hiked slowly back up to Tom Leonard Shelter, where we had lunch on the deck. Then I packed, said good-bye and headed south down the trail, deep in thought. I prayed most of the day. The trail meandered along the ridge line of East Mountain and headed down into the valley. A four-mile road walk took me to where the historic battle of Shay's Rebellion took place. Farmers, concerned that heavy taxes were causing some of them to lose their land holdings, had revolted against the local government. The last clash in the uprising led by Daniel Shay was fought in a field along South Egremont Road in Sheffield, Massachusetts. The trail crossed many more fields and came out along Jug End Road near a great campsite with a refreshing piped-in spring. When I arrived, I was greeted by nine boys and two counselors from a school in nearby Litchfield. That night we had a great time together by a campfire.

The next day's hike from Jug End Road took me over seven mountainous bumps. After four miles I reached the fire tower on the 2,602-foot summit of Mt. Everett. The trail then crossed a magnificent ridge that resembled a cliff walk for two miles. From that vantage point I could see southern Massachusetts and the Connecticut Valley. After climbing over Race Mountain, the trail took a turn to the west for a mile into a cool beautiful place called Sages Ravine. I rested at a wonderful brook side campsite, then made the steep ascent of 2,316-foot Bear Mountain, on top of which is a stone monument giving visitors a 360-degree view of southern New England. In the clear light of a late autumn afternoon, I came down Bear Mountain and headed for Bond Shelter, about a mile and a half south on the Appalachian Trail.

Massachusetts

The trail travels by the field in which the last battle of Shay's Rebellion was fought. In 1787 farmers in debt rebelled against heavy taxation and state seizure of property.

The Appalachian Trail follows the Housatonic River for many glorious miles.

Meandering Along the Housatonic River

Connecticut

When I arrived at Bond Shelter, the weather turned cold. As the winds picked up in velocity, I put on all the clothing in my pack and made two cups of soup and a favorite meal, scalloped potatoes. The wind was so cold and fierce that I set up my tent in the shelter. As night fell, there seemed to be voices in the wind. At 3 a.m. I was awakened by distant howling. I had never heard coyotes or wild dogs except on television or in the movies, and as the howling drew nearer and continued for more than an hour, I became nervous. *"God, you are my protection from all danger."* At times the animal sounds seemed close. Then they were far away. The thermometer on my pack read 35 degrees, the coldest I had experienced in camping out. I wondered how cold it was for northbounders still on the trail in Maine.

"God's greatness can be seen in the wilderness. As I look intently at creation, I see that God must be even more magnificent. The balance of hills, valleys, streams, woods, ferns, trees, plants and seedlings — all depending upon and living in harmony with one another — is awesome. Nature is truly in balance, and I feel God wants me to learn from this example. I need to be balanced in my own life and with Him. If I live only for myself, what purpose do I really have? As plants and animals live in perfect harmony, I pray that throughout my life I will be able to live with others in perfect peace."

The next morning I started hiking early, dressed in layers of clothing, but after a mile I warmed up and was able to remove some clothes. The hike through forests near Salisbury, Connecticut was beautiful. I had a contemplative lunch at Limestone Spring Lean-

White 2x6-inch blazes on posts and trees became my constant guide along the trail.

to. In the trail register I saw that Bill (Sprained-Rice) O'Brian had stayed there the night before. Being a close friend of Molly and Geoff, he needed to get out into the wilderness and sort out his feelings, and he had written a long eulogy for the couple in the register. Reading this left me deep in thought and prayer. After drinking from the cold spring, I continued down the trail through the Housatonic State Forest and onto the ridge leading to 1,390-foot Easter Mountain. I hiked more than 18 miles, the last one difficult, catching up with Jim at Pine Brook Swamp Shelter just as another storm came in. It rained hard all night long.

> Let all nature rejoice in the presence of God.
> Be mindful that He holds everything in the palm
>   of His hand.
> If He calls us home, to dust we return.
> But true joy and peace come when we trust in Him fully.
> This is our holy call.

The next seven miles to the magnificent Silver Hill Cabin were beautiful. The trail rambled over hills and brooks. The weather turned cooler, and the bugs finally disappeared. This picturesque countryside cabin in the woods, with its mountain views, running water and fireplace, made me feel as if I was in someone's personal mountain hideaway. Early in the evening, as Jim and I were preparing to light a fire in the fireplace, Hob and Deb (The Tandem Teachers) paid me a surprise visit. They had heard that I would probably be there for a day's rest and had brought delicious red apples and other goodies. It had been a great day on the trail, and I thanked God for good friends. I was able to spend Rosh HaShanah with Hob and Deb. Rosh HaShanah is New Year's day, when Jews all over the world hear the blowing of a ram's horn called a shofar. When we got into Hob and Deb's car, they blew the horn loud and long all through the hills near the quiet village of Cornwall Bridge. Late in the afternoon The Tandem Teachers left, and I sat on the deck of the cabin watching the sun slowly melt into the peaceful countryside.

> As the New Year begins in awe and wonder,
> My heart is turned to you, O King.
> I can only be holy if Your presence lives in me.
> As the seasons change and grow, I must do the same.
> So change me, Lord, to your image and will,
> Let my life be satisfied, holy and fulfilled.
> Just let me hear your sweet, gentle voice, O Lord,
> And all the rivers of life I'll be able to ford.
> With your strength and wisdom to guide me,
> Love, joy and peace for each new day I will surely see.

As I left Silver Hill Shelter, a heavy fog hung over the valley, extending to the shore of the Housatonic River. It was wonderful to walk on a wide flat dirt path along the river for more than five glorious miles. Mist rising left delicate drops of water on spider webs hanging from plants at the river's edge. The trail eventually headed north and climbed St. Johns Ledges for half a mile, then followed the ridge to Caleb's Peak, across Fuller Mountain and down to the road near Kent. Sondra met me there so we could drive to Glens Falls in upstate New York to watch the largest hot air balloon festival in the Northeast. It was a blessing to see my sister Sharon, nephew Adam, niece Abbe, Sondra's mom Madlyn and her Aunt Pansy. It rained most of the following day, and the balloons did not lift off, so we spent time eating and talking about life and the trail. At times it was difficult for me to be thrust into the crowded world of buildings, cars and the bustle of life. I yearned to be back on the trail. The next morning was picture-perfect, and my sister and Sondra flew high into the sky with a hundred other multi-colored balloons. After looking around the Lake George area with my family and friends, we left in the late afternoon and drove back to Kent. We stayed in a local inn so I could get on the trail early the next morning.

It was another cool refreshing day as I hiked from Connecticut into New York. In a few spots the trail wiggled along ridges in the Schaghticoke Mountain Indian Reservations into New York and then swung back into Connecticut along the Housatonic River. After following the river for more than a mile, I came to the wide meadow that encompasses the Ten Mile River Campsite – where the Ten Mile River joins the Housatonic. After crossing the river, I climbed the 1,000-foot Ten Mile Mountain and walked down into New York. It was near the end of September and 720 miles of the Appalachian Trail were behind me as I said good-bye to New England.

The Appalachian Trail meanders through beautiful forests on Sharon Mountain in the Housatonic State Forest, CT.

I spent a wonderful Sabbath evening and day with Hob and Deb (The Tandem Teachers) and Jim in the luxurious Silver Hill Shelter near Cornwall Bridge, CT.

The trail was ablaze in flowers as I climbed Hosner Mountain in New York.

New York

The Appalachian Trail's Oldest Section

New York

The trail into New York traveled along country roads through forested hills. When I arrived at Webatuck Shelter, I was surprised to see Rueven again. He was not feeling well, but we chatted for a while, and then I continued south over Hammersley Ridge, coming down to a road crossing near the Appalachian Trail Railroad Station, a stop on the Metro-North Commuter Railroad. A person living in New York City can go to Grand Central Station, take a train, step off at this station and then hike to either Georgia or Maine! In 17 miles I came to a beautiful spot at the edge of a meadow near a quiet stream. I should have camped there but decided to push on to Telephone Pioneers Shelter. This added four miles to my hike. When I awoke the next morning, the sun's rays were shining over the horizon through a mist. Leaning against the shelter wall, I was filled with a tremendous peace. I dreamily watched the fiery ball of the sun rise higher into the sky and burn off the rising mist. I wrote:

Appalachian Trail Station, a stop on the Metro-North Commuter Railroad, can take you to Grand Central Station in New York City.

> With the sun rising over the mountains
> And the gentle mist floating across the valleys,
> We can see the powerful hand of God.
> With the quiet calling of the birds
> And the rustling of the changing leaves,
> We can begin to hear the still, small voice of God.
> In the tranquil coolness of the early morning
> The fresh scent of the mountain air fills our nostrils.
> All senses become attuned to the One who created it all.
> As we touch the trees and feel the flowing life of nature,

The autumn foliage was coming out at the beginning of October on Little Dam Lake, NY.

Our lives have become intermingled with everything.
We can feel the awesome presence of God
And taste and see that God is sweet and compassionate.

"The stillness that pervades the wilderness flowed gently around me."

"To be obedient and listen to what God is telling me is the key to life, but it seems I sometimes must learn lessons through pain and discipline. I can become so entrenched in my ways that God, at times, needs to use drastic measures to turn me around, to change me and mold me into His image. I am clay, and He is the master potter. Do I dare pray: 'Change me, O Lord, mold me. Break off pieces of the pot that don't fit well, O Lord, and remold me so I can become a whole vessel.' Can I change? Can my heart be purged through the fire (as gold is purified) and come out pure? I want to be like you, O Lord, and have your qualities radiating from my life. I want to serve and honor you with all my being. So continue your work in my life, Father God, and change me. Let me see the error of my ways that I might repent of them and be changed forever."

Exhaustion

The daily physical pain and mental exertion of a thru-hike were difficult. I had struggled to get to Pioneer Telephone Shelter, and now, at the beginning of a new day's journey, I was already tired. It was awesome to be hiking alone almost every day. There were few people on the trail now, so my reliance on God for strength was deepening. I tried to reach Ralph's Peak Hiker Cabin but was drained of energy as I hiked along Pawling Mountain and Nuclear Lake. Perhaps the leaking of low level radiation, which supposedly existed there, zapped me. (Actually, no significant levels of radiation have been found in that area since a nuclear facility near the lake was closed in 1972.)

The trail continued south over Depot Hill, then crossed Interstate 84 in Connecticut and went up Hosner Mountain. At this point, overcome with fatigue, I had to camp at Bailey Spring, about three miles from the hiker's cabin. After hiking to the ridge crest on Hosner Mountain, I came to the blue-blazed side trail to Bailey Springs Campsite. In the next half mile the trail descended steeply for several hundred vertical feet and was within a quarter of a mile of the noisy highway. The campsite was dirty and damp, the only drinking water coming from a stagnant pool, and hordes of mosquitoes added to the annoyance of traffic noise. I was not happy as I settled into my tent, exhausted, and listened to the drone of trucks and cars all night long.

Awake early, I began my second ascent of Hosner Mountain. Along the side trail I photographed ferns that were turning to lovely autumn colors. I then hiked three miles over the mountain, crossed the busy Taconic State Parkway and headed for Ralph's Peak Hiker Cabin. I stayed there for a while looking at paraphernalia left over the years by hikers and the caretaker. The

trail then climbed Shenandoah Mountain and passed Canopus Lake in Fahnestock State Park. For the first time on the trip, I felt a little lonely, having seen no one for three days in a row. Also, after hiking ten miles my feet were hurting again, but I continued to Dennytown Campsite, where I saw three beautiful white-tailed deer prancing through the meadow as I set up my tent. The well water was rusty, but I was thirsty and thankful for it. As I slept in my tent, I was frequently awakened by hungry raccoons. I kept shooing them away during the night – and even put my boots inside so they would not be eaten.

"As I walked in silence today, I heard the sounds of nature. Although distracting thoughts tried to rush in like a mighty wind and charge upon the open fields of my mind, the stillness that pervades the wilderness flowed gently around me, and eventually I found my mind quieted to a point where I could set my heart and spirit to hear God. To hear the sounds of nature – crickets chirping, birds singing, the wind whispering, leaves rustling, sticks cracking, streams gurgling – and to listen, to walk in silence alone, to shut out all voices but God's... that was what I wanted, and indeed His voice was the clearest and rose above the tumult."

The trail followed ridges in the Putnam Valley, crossing many hills, and eventually descended to the Graymoor Monastery, which is nine miles from the Dennytown Campsite. After three days alone I arrived at this Franciscan retreat where for more than 20 years thru-hikers have stayed the night. Met by a monk named Rafael, I was taken to a dormitory wing in which I was the only visitor. In looking through the register, I noticed that Pig Pen, Speed and The Beastmaster had somehow passed me and were now several days ahead of me. After a short chapel service the monks served a great dinner, and I talked with Brother Anthony. This was truly a place to rest and reflect. At breakfast the next morning, Brother Anthony and Rafael kept telling jokes. It was a joyful time for me.

Leaving by 9 a.m, I hiked six and a half miles over many hills down to the widest river crossing on the Appalachian Trail. The Hudson River is more than half a mile wide at this point, and, at 124 feet above sea level, is the trail's lowest elevation. I crossed the river on the Bear Mountain Bridge, which in times past charged a ten-cent toll for hikers. Half way across the bridge I noticed two figures walking toward me. To my great surprise, my brothers Gary and Richard had come to take me home for another Jewish holiday, Yom Kippur. We laughed and talked as we went through the Trailside Museum and Zoo, following the Appalachian Trail to the Bear Mountain Inn. Then packed everything into my brother's car for the drive north to Massachusetts.

On Yom Kippur, the Day of Atonement, Jews fast as a sign of repentance and God's forgiveness for sins of the old year and His blessing for the new year. This was a wonderful time with my family. I knew it would be the last time I would see them until the end of my journey. While I was home, I reorganized mail drop boxes, putting more photographic film in some of them, and again visited my 100-year-old Grandpa Joe, who lives near Boston.

As I awoke on the deck of Telephone Pioneers Shelter in New York, the sun was just coming over the horizon.

Appalachian Trail sign near Canopus Lake, NY.

White Appalachian Trail blazes dot the rocky ridge of Shenandoah Mountain near Fahnestock State Park, NY.

New York

The first section of the Appalachian Trail was completed in Bear Mountain State Park, NY.

The Bear Mountain Bridge span of Hudson River is the lowest elevation and widest river crossing on the Appalachian Trail.

"Traveling between the wilderness and society felt like an emotional roller coaster."

Gary and I drove Rich to the airport before returning to climb Bear Mountain. The first part of the Appalachian Trail was constructed on Bear Mountain in Harriman State Park in 1923. Gary and I climbed to the 1,305-foot summit in a few hours and rested with tourists who drove up. The trail descended through the woods and connected with the mountain's auto road. As it began to rain, I sadly said good-bye to Gary, who would walk down the road to the base of the mountain while I hiked into the woods and then over West Mountain. It was so late in the day that I would never make the five and a half miles to the next shelter before dark, so I planned to camp along the trail using water I was carrying from the Bear Mountain summit. Eventually, as drizzle turned to rain, I found a good place for my tent and settled in, thinking of my family and the challenging journey that still lay before me.

Refreshment

The next morning was beautiful and sunny. I took my time heading over West Mountain and crossing the Palisades Parkway. As I hiked up Black Mountain and 1,195-foot Letterrock Mountain, my body and feet felt as if they were starting the entire journey again, and it was amazing to see what a few days off did to my psyche. Traveling between the wilderness and society felt like an emotional roller coaster. In the 10-plus miles to Fingerboard Mountain Shelter, I saw many flocks of Canada geese flying south. Unfortunately, the shelter had no water, and I had to hike a half mile downhill to fill my bag from Lake Tiorati. The water had things floating and moving in it, so I boiled it for dinner and purified the rest with iodine crystals. Again I realized that a southbounder's journey is a solitary one. Autumn was coming into fullness, and though there was great beauty on the trail, few people were hiking. With God's help I was learning to rely more on myself.

The next day's 15 miles took me over rough terrain including five mountain tops. When I came to Mombasha High Point at 1,262 feet, I did not know if I could make the next four miles to Bellvale Mountain Campsite. I sat on the summit and gazed at the New York City skyline, barely discernible on the horizon, and dreamed of water since there was so little of it on the trail. Then, slowly, I hiked two miles down to Fitzgerald Falls and gorged myself on water, debating whether to camp there or continue two miles to the campsite on the ridge. Because the falls were close to the road, I decided to try for the campsite before dark. Physically and spiritually weary, I prayed that God would send someone for me to talk with, especially about spiritual matters. After struggling to reach the ridge, I walked more than a mile before arriving at the blue-blazed campsite trail. On this I came to a well with a hand pump and refilled my water bottles.

New York

Farther down, near the campsite, I heard voices and saw a roaring fire with four men around it chatting. Wandering over, I learned that Jim, Norm, Walter and Ken were from Ohio, and from their words and joyful manner, I realized within minutes that they had a deep, solid faith in Jesus. When we discovered our common relationship with God, there was great rejoicing, and we talked and sang late into the night under a starry sky. After the others went to their tents, Ken and I talked past midnight and would have gone longer had not the others yelled at us good-naturedly to turn in. What a joy this was! My soul and spirit were fully refreshed. After breakfast the next morning we prayed for each other before heading in opposite directions on the trail. Through continued contact since that time, I have become close friends with each of these men. If I had camped alone by the falls and left early the next day, I would have missed this divine encounter with wonderful Christians and the rich associations that have come of it.

In hiking along the ridge, I came across a couple camped in a homemade shelter on the trail above Greenwood Lake. Moving south on the Appalachian Trail, they planned to walk east toward Washington, D.C. to be at the Vietnam Memorial for Veteran's Day. Clay had served as a front man in Vietnam. It was a dangerous job, and most of his friends had perished. In a few hours of talking over coffee, I learned of Clay's war experiences. They were beyond comprehension. One day behind enemy lines, his platoon was ambushed, and he was the only survivor. I prayed that God would bless him and Liz on their journeys in life.

I continued on the Bellvale Mountain ridge for three miles. At Bearfort Mountain the trail turned sharply away from the ridge and headed toward New Jersey, weaving through the autumn-colored forest and within four miles coming to Wawayanda State Park. With the park closed for the season, I had to walk another half mile to a farm stand for water. I bought a couple of apples and some vegetables there, and when I got back to my tent, it was dark. I cooked dinner, thankful to God for the chance to walk in this wonderful wilderness. The next day was a Sabbath, and I stayed around the campsite, walking the shore of Parker Lake. It rained in the afternoon, so I retreated to my tent for the remainder of the day and night. It was a greatly needed rest. *"My feet still give me a great deal of pain. Although I have hiked 820 miles, I struggle after hiking just seven miles. I believe God is letting me know that it is not by my strength that I will reach the end of this journey, but by His. I humble myself before Him and pray that He will lift me up when I am down."*

Long before dawn the next day I left the campsite in fog. A full moon gave the countryside a serene beauty, and I hiked about four miles before turning off my head lamp. The trail followed old country roads to the end of the Wawayanda Mountain ridge, then descended into fields and pastures. As I came out of a field onto Vernon Valley Road, I met a 75-year-old man named John Card – a

"You were much too quiet," he said. "I thought you were a deer."

Gideon and a dairy farmer who had 11 children – and after walking together for a while he invited me to church in Sussex the following Sunday. I continued over Pochuck Mountain, coming into the wide valley that holds Unionville, New York, my next trail town. I reached the post office by 3 p.m., having hiked 18 miles. I sent out letters and film and mailed extra food to Delaware Water Gap, Pennsylvania. Rick, the owner of the Unionville Inn, let me set up my tent on a second-story porch. Then I took a long shower and went downstairs for a delicious dinner of chicken with raspberry cream sauce, soup and homemade cheesecake. The next morning I slept late and walked around the town talking to people. I also read in the Bible and wrote in my journal. After a late night in the pub, eating pizza and listening to a pleasant singer named Wayne, I retired for a restful sleep.

I awoke early enough to meet John by 7 a.m. At his church I gave a short talk about my journey, then had lunch with his family. He had built his own street in Sussex, and many of his children were living on it. In the afternoon John took me to the trail near the center of town, and I walked through the Kittatinny Valley and up to High Point Shelter on Kittatinny Mountain. On the way I had my first experience with a hunter. After crossing a small brook, the trail headed into woods and turned to the left. As I made that turn, a voice from above startled me. A teen-aged boy, camouflaged, had been sitting on a tree branch 20 feet above the ground. He was staring intently at me, a bow in hand with an arrow drawn. "You were much too quiet," he said. "I thought you were a deer." Shaken by this encounter, I continued walking to higher ground. To dry it out from the morning's dew, I set my tent up inside the shelter and had a late-night dinner of hot chocolate and rice pilaf.

I met Ken, Walter, Norm, and Jim at the Bellvale Mountain Campsite. They were on their 17th year of hiking the Appalachian Trail and made it to New York from Georgia.

High Point Monument stands on the highest mountain in New Jersey.

Touches of Autumn

New Jersey

The trail from the shelter on Kittatinny Mountain took me to a 1,803-foot knoll in High Point State Park – the highest elevation in New Jersey. On the way there I met a few people on the trail and sat on Sunrise Mountain, looking over the northern New Jersey countryside. At the park visitor's center I met a great ranger, Ed Pomeroy, who gave me a cup of coffee and talked with me for quite a while. Then I hiked two miles to Gren Anderson Shelter, where I spent the night. Leaving early in the morning, I traveled along Kittatinny Ridge again, down to Culver's Gap, then climbed the ridge heading south over Rattlesnake Mountain to Flatbrookville and Millbrook Road. This section of trail on high mountain roads was beautiful, and I had time to enjoy looking around instead of constantly looking at my feet to avoid tripping over roots and rocks.

"Today was hard. My feet hurt most of the time. I did not realize how far I had hiked until I arrived at Rattlesnake Spring, which is 17.7 miles from Gren Anderson Shelter. For those last five miles to the spring in the early afternoon, I had to take my boots off and put on my sneakers. I filled my two-gallon water bag with delicious water and walked to a field near the spring to set up camp. The sun was just setting, and I ate dinner here in the tent as night fell. Earlier a big fat raccoon was hanging around, sniffing at my backpack. He got my garbage bag and dragged it off a little ways, but he eventually left, and it's a good thing because I needed to sleep. The trail is getting rockier and rougher each day. Many godly men and women have had their faith tested, and I feel that is happening to me now."

The next morning dawned in a heavy fog. I hiked along a beautiful ridge to Sunfish Pond, the southernmost glacial lake on

After getting water from Rattlesnake Spring, I looked up and saw this beautiful fern bursting with color.

the trail, and just north of the Delaware Water Gap I came into Worthington State Forest. On the ridge I met an official bird watcher for the state of New Jersey, whose job was to count various kinds of birds making their annual pilgrimage south. Kittatinny Mountain creates wonderful updrafts of wind for many miles, and birds have easy flying in that area. I saw a number of hawks, eagles and other birds through the man's telescope. Then, ending a 13 and a half mile day, I came down the long ridge into Delaware Water Gap and crossed the bridge into Pennsylvania. In the past few days the weather had been gorgeous, almost like summer.

View of Northern New Jersey from Black Mountain.

New Jersey

The Appalachian Trail is covered in fog on Kittatinny Mountain, NJ.

The trail on Blue Mountain near Lehigh Gap follows a ridge scarred by an old zinc-smelting plant in the valley below. As the autumn came into its glory, mountain grasses glowed in golden hues.

Legendary Rocks of Pennsylvania

Pennsylvania

Crossing the Delaware River marked 880 miles that I had hiked in a hundred days. It was the middle of October, and I was behind schedule but thankful to have come this far. At the Presbyterian Church of the Mountain in Delaware Water Gap, I was greeted by pastor Karen Nichols. We talked for awhile before I settled into the basement hostel for the evening – the only hiker staying there that night. Sondra came for a visit, and in the morning we shopped, ate at all-you-can-eat restaurants and visited beautiful waterfalls in the area. We talked with Karen for hours that afternoon. It was a wonderful time of fellowship.

I was up early for my first hike in Pennsylvania, having heard that this was one of the most arduous segments of the Appalachian Trail on account of small, tightly packed pyramid-shaped rocks. Legend had it that Pennsylvania trail volunteers sharpened these rocks each year. I did not know what to expect until I saw these rocks and began teetering among them and twisting my ankles. Fortunately, the trail followed fairly flat ridge lines, dropping into gaps now and again and then returning to the heights. In a rough section called Wolf Rocks I lost my way a few times because the terrain was similar in all directions. Autumn leaves were coming into their glory, and I shot two rolls of film there. In 15 miles the trail descended to Wind Gap, where Sondra and I stayed for another Sabbath. It was a relaxed day with a lot of eating and driving through the Pennsylvania countryside.

I left late the next morning with an exceptionally heavy pack and climbed Blue Mountain. Because the rocks were hurting

The morning after the huge storm, the Appalachian Trail on Blue Mountain was flooded with water for miles.

The Pinnacle overlooks the Pennsylvania countryside and miles of farmland.

"I'm in a river! water three to four inches deep with sticks and leaves floating on it is flowing swiftly around my tent."

my already sore feet, I could go only nine miles. I settled in early, placing my tent right on the trail next to John and Linda's Blue Mountain Mailbox and Register. In the morning I set out for Lehigh Gap. As I neared the town, the landscape changed dramatically. Years ago poisonous smoke from a zinc processing plant in the valley killed most of the mountainside vegetation, and the area was bleak and bare. Then the trail pitched steeply into a rock field leading to a bridge over the Lehigh River. I climbed out of the gap onto the ridge and hiked to Bake Oven Knob Shelter. It had been a strenuous 20-mile day. I arrived about an hour before dark, took a T-shirt bath in the spring and ate dinner as the sun set at the edge of beautiful wilderness. I could tell the days were getting shorter because I was arriving at the shelters closer to dusk. Noting this, I wondered what would happen to my progress in December.

Mice

The next day I hiked another 20 miles to Eckville Hostel. Following the Blue Mountain Ridge in Pennsylvania, the Appalachian Trail is a major migratory route for birds. On the ridge at Pine Knob and Bears Rocks, I met bird watchers who had seen 800 starlings, 50 red-tailed hawks and many falcons and eagles the previous day. The rocks were still hard on my feet as I hiked through the bird sanctuary on Hawk Mountain – a place where on one day in September in the early 1970s birders saw more than 21,000 raptors! The trail was so hard on my feet that my second pair of boots was falling apart. I was thankful when I found the hostel open on a cold night. With a fire going in the wood-burning stove, it was 40 degrees warmer inside than out. Although I was alone that night, I did have a lot of "company" because the hostel had mice. Actually, there were mice in almost every shelter on the trail. Once I got used to them, I considered them cute, but at times they could be bothersome. They usually came out at night, hungry, so I had to hang my food by strings on shelter ceilings. If I left food in my pack, the mice would gnaw holes in it. They would also crawl on me. After a while I began carrying extra sunflower seeds to throw on the floor away from where I was sleeping. This kept the critters busy until the wee hours at least. *"For the first time I feel like a hermit. It is lonely, but I don't mind it so much now. I know God has called me to seek Him, and being alone with Him is surely part of this journey. I thank you, God, for filling this quiet cabin with peace and your presence."*

Big Mistake

The stars were shining when I awoke the next morning and got a fire going. After a breakfast of instant oatmeal and a bagel with peanut butter and jelly, I climbed the

next ridge to The Pinnacle, a place that has great views of the countryside. Along the way I met Don, a man who gathers honey for a living. He was taking a break from his labors. The trail then took me to another beautiful vista called Pulpit Rock, which overlooks Blue Rocks, a dry mile-long river bed filled with large boulders. There I met three boys from Philadelphia and Lisa, whose trail name was The Three Amigos. She had hiked from Georgia to Pennsylvania that year with her two dogs, Kliban and Maude, and she was trying to finish Pennsylvania in day trips, hoping to complete the trail in the following years. We talked for a while, and she told me that if I ever needed help in Pennsylvania, I could call her. It was then 15 and a half miles over a hilly ridge down to the valley and Port Clinton, a town that has an outdoor pavilion where hikers can stay. There was no water there, but a town resident gave me some as I walked down the street. My feet were sore and forming more blisters.

Traffic noise gave me unsettled sleep in the pavilion. It was a steep mile to the Blue Mountain ridge in the morning, and my feet started to hurt four miles later. Also, the wind picked up. From somewhere in the valley I heard a long siren (a sound that usually meant it was noon), and I was still 15 or more miles to the 501 Shelter. Unwisely, I passed by the side trail to Eagles Nest Shelter and decided to go on. A bit later when I paused to eat a sandwich I bought in Port Clinton, the wind sharpened, clouds turned dark and the temperature dropped.

I was still 11 miles from 501 Shelter when it began to rain. I should have backtracked, but I hurried on for four more miles. My feet were giving out and my stomach was aching when I decided to take the side trail to Black Swatara Spring. I hiked 500 yards to the spring and filled my water bag and in so doing saw where someone had set a tent. It was raining hard as I hastily erected my own tent and threw the things I would need for the night into it. Lightning flashed constantly overhead. I had never seen rain so heavy. I skipped dinner to wait out the storm.

"What a day!!! Lord, have mercy on me! Here I am sitting in my tent with winds gusting to 50 m.p.h. It has been raining for three or four hours. I thought I could make it. I passed a great shelter, Eagles Nest, about five miles ago, thinking I could do the full 22 to the 501 Shelter. Man, is it pouring out!!!! The tent floor is bouncing like a swimming pool cover. I have never seen it going up and down like this. I can't understand why it is happening. Oh, no! Even though it is pouring out, I have opened the door to peer into the darkness with my head lamp. I can't believe it. I'm in a river! Water three to four inches deep with sticks and leaves floating on it is flowing swiftly around my tent. I have now closed the door and am praying for protection and safety for the night. I can't believe water has not come into my Moss tent yet as I sit on this waterbed."

Despite all this excitement, I felt sure God had me safely in the palm of His hand, and eventually the water moving under and around me lulled me to sleep. During the night the storm quieted.

After heavy rains the Conodoguinet River overflowed onto the Appalachian Trail.

The Eckville Hostel contained a wood-burning stove and outside hand pump for water. Mice were my only company for the night.

I got stuck in a severe thunderstorm and had to camp off the trail near Black Swatara Spring. Unfortunately, the campsite became a stream, and water flowed around my tent all night long.

The Appalachian Trail crosses the 20-mile wide Cumberland Valley in Pennsylvania. Much of the trail in this area goes through fertile farm and pasture land.

"The forest looked and smelled delightful from all the life-giving water, and I felt richly refreshed."

I awoke to a mixture of clouds and sun with a stiff westerly breeze. As I exited the tent, I saw that a stream had indeed flowed under my tent and was still flowing. The trail leading to the spring had become a flowing river in the downpour. It flowed right into the little campsite and then down the mountainside. That day I walked more than two and a half miles in water. The trail was flooded, and there was no other way but to walk through it. In places the water was more than a foot deep, and at times the forest floor was like a lake. My drenched boots were coming further apart, and I wondered how I could keep walking across miles of rocks. Some rocks were pointed, slippery, jagged, and tilting. Others were large and rounded or knife sharp and craggy.

On my way I stopped and talked to two grouse hunters. It was 40 degrees and very windy. As I came by a beautiful waterfall and tent site area, I met hikers who worked for the Teen Challenge ministry in Rehearsburg. Terry and Doug invited me to camp with them, but I wanted to get to the 501 Shelter for a Sabbath rest, which my feet and spirit needed. At the shelter I bought two Klondike bars from George, the caretaker, whose house was close by, and had a great night's sleep.

It was 30 degrees in the shelter in the morning, so I stayed in my toasty sleeping bag reading the Bible and writing. Suddenly Terry and Doug popped in. They had planned to continue hiking but came back just to take me to the farm and school in Rehearsburg. We ate breakfast, stored most of our gear in George's shack and began a leisurely descent into the valley. That night we slept in an empty house on the Teen Challenge campus, and I felt fortunate to be in God's presence and peace. At church in the morning I talked with the ministry's director, Sonny Oliver, and after a filling meal Doug and Terry drove me back to the trail. I was refreshed, but since it was late, I decided to spend another night at the 501 Shelter.

Boot Problems

In the morning the ridge was foggy. I felt peaceful and contemplative as I walked along in the heavy mist, sensing nature's stillness. My feet hurt after only eight miles. I descended into Swatara Gap, then went up into the hills and onto a two-mile country road to the Green Country Store, where I bought bread, jelly, soda and pastry and then called Lisa (The Three Amigos). I like to be independent, relying on God to meet my needs, but at times I must rely on people God places in my life. My feet had more blisters than they did in Hanover, New Hampshire, 500 miles back up the trail. My call found Lisa at home, and we arranged to meet a few days down the trail. She would pick me up and help me get new boots. It was raining as I

126

Pennsylvania

left the store for the four-mile walk to Rausch Gap Shelter. Sitting up against the wooden back of the shelter in my sleeping bag, feeling the nip in the air and gazing out at the heavy rain, I felt a longing in my heart for home – a warm bed and family. The sound of rain on the metal roof lulled me to sleep.

It was raining hard when I headed south again in the morning. My Gore-Tex suit was put to the test as I hiked through St. Anthony's Wilderness along Sharp Mountain. I traveled past the ruins of a village with stone foundations still showing in the woods. The trail became a full stream in so many places that I could hardly walk. One creek became a roaring river four feet deep. It took a long time to find a proper place, but I finally crossed it by facing upstream and using my staff for balance. Alone and walking in the downpour, I truly enjoyed the day. The forest looked and smelled delightful from all the life-giving water, and I felt richly refreshed. Sitting briefly in Peter's Mountain Shelter, I was filled with awe and joy in the Lord. Moisture laden clouds floated through the shelter, making it like a cool sauna. The trail traversed the Peter's Mountain ridge for seven miles before descending steeply to the Susquehana River and crossing on Clark's Ferry Bridge into Duncannon. The 450-mile Susquehana is the longest river the Appalachian Trail crosses. As I walked Duncannon's quaint streets, I met two nice ladies talking on their lawns and visited the Doyle Hotel, where I gobbled two hamburgers and fries and drank a couple of Cokes. It was a long 20-mile day with a two-hour stop for mail in Duncannon.

I almost stepped on this box turtle, which was right on the trail. The creature was courteous enough to let me take a picture of it.

"It was a bit too much, but I'm glad I'm out here in the wilderness instead of staying in the town. The storm cleared overnight, and the winds softened. The ridge walk leading out of Duncannon was beautiful. I love the forest after rain. Everything is so fresh and clean. Rain is life to the forest as water is life to us. All in all, yesterday was lovely. The rain, the sweet smells, the autumn leaves in their colorful display, rivers of flowing water and the glory of walking through the clouds along the ridge filled my senses with wonder at God's perfect creation. As I yield to God, He guides me into more truth and knowledge, leading me on paths of splendor. Communing with Him, I see the glory in nature's beauty. O Lord, you are always with me, and by your Spirit living within, you guide me in love. From dawn to twilight you disclose your eternal truths. You have filled my heart with joy and my mind with wisdom to serve you more faithfully. You are all that I desire. You have picked me up when I have fallen and strengthened me when I was weak. I will seek you daily for a pure heart and for your awesome presence in all of my life."

The Appalachian Trail Conference has hundreds of volunteers who help maintain the trail. They clear away debris and overgrowth, check the shelters, adopt parts of the trail, and build new trails and shelters. This crew is volunteering a week of their time to build a new bridge over a creek that drains into the Conodoguinet River.

Because my feet were hurting so, I had second thoughts about pushing on. Not only were the soles of my boots de-laminating, but the inside padded leather had worn away to the hard outer leather. There were huge blisters on the backs of my feet. After ascending to the ridge of Cove Mountain above Duncannon, the trail became rocky again, which made the situation even more

Before reaching Wind Gap, the Appalachian Trail winds for miles over ankle-twisting rocks along the Kittatinny Mountain ridge.

Hebeloma mushrooms were growing right on the trail as I climbed up to Wolfs Rocks, PA.

"Parts of the trail were now completely submerged."

difficult. I was trying to make it to a campsite where there was a spring, but I could make it only to a stream at the bottom of the ridge. At dusk I set up my tent and cooked a rice dinner. *"Here I am, truly in the wilderness by a beautiful stream! The stars are out. The crickets are chirping. There are no bugs, and deer are walking around nearby. Thank you, Lord."*

I awoke in the stillness of dawn, broke camp and headed over a ridge before descending into the Cumberland Valley. Entering the area through fields of cows and corn along the Conodoguinet Creek, I came upon a volunteer trail crew working on a log bridge. They told me what time it was. I knew my pace had slowed because of the pain in my feet, and I would be late for my rendezvous with Lisa. From the previous day's heavy rains Conodoguinet Creek had become a swollen river. Parts of the trail were now completely submerged, and portions of it that had been under water were now a muddy mess. Eventually, while walking in sticky mud-laden boots through a pasture, I had to stop and put on my sneakers. I was beginning to get angry at myself for making Lisa wait for hours. I even tried jogging through a few cornfields and cow pastures to get to Route 641, which was still two and a half miles away.

When I arrived at the meeting place, Lisa was not there, and I did not blame her for not waiting. I sat around for a while to see if she would show up. She had gone to another road crossing, thinking I might be there since I was not at Route 641 at the appointed time. It was a tremendous relief to me, in a short while, to see her pull up in her pick-up. We drove immediately to a store where I bought a pair of Vasque Summit hiking boots. My feet are size 12, and the store's largest pair was an eleven and a half, but I took them anyway. They were made of medium-weight Gortex leather. The boots I had been wearing were also leather but a pound heavier each and twice as expensive. Lisa took me to her friend Steve's house, where we had a wonderful meal and talked late.

My feet expanded each night from the pressure that hiking put on them during the day, so when I put on the boots the next morning, my toes were scrunched. I was thankful that I did not do a lot of walking in them the previous day. We went back to the mall to exchange them, then drove to Wildware Outfitters, which had a larger pair of Summits. As a cold north wind blew in, we drove to Route 641 with some of my gear so I could test the boots. I hiked five miles of beautiful farmland to Boiling Springs and spent time talking to ladies working in the regional office for the Appalachian Trail Conference. The boots felt much better and lighter. Lisa picked me up at the ATC office in the late afternoon and took me back to Steve's house, where I wrote postcards, packaged my old boots to be shipped home and organized my gear. I decided to spend the Sabbath at Steve's house. While Steve hunted wild

turkey and Lisa ran errands, I relaxed and played with Lisa's dogs. Later the three of us had a great time talking, and Steve cooked a wonderful venison dinner.

Lessons in the Leaves

*A*fter a filling pancake breakfast I got going again, leaving Boiling Springs along a duck-filled waterway and passing through cornfields before getting up out of the valley. The trail ascended Center Point Knob, where a monument marks the original midpoint of the Appalachian Trail, and from there I hiked the ridge to the Alec Kennedy Shelter – where, surprisingly, Rueven had been waiting for me. He was a sight to be seen. Wanting to make sure he would not get shot by hunters, he was now clad from head to toe in bright orange clothing. We talked for awhile, and he said he hoped we could meet for the next Sabbath. Deer season had truly begun. While hiking I had seen a few hunters from the trail and heard a number of gun shots in the distance. That day I hiked nine miles over two small peaks to Tagg Run Shelters.

"Autumn is still in full bloom, and nature is beginning to shut down. The soil is covered with a carpet of colors turning brown, promising to bring forth new life in the future. I want to flow with God's seasons in my own life. Letting go of old ways in my life seems, in a way, like the process of green leaves turning brown in autumn and dying. Then, just as potential new plant growth lies dormant in winter, I trust in and wait for change and spiritual growth to become evident in the spring with new life. In summer, I can mature, ever growing, strengthening, and moving steadily forward in my walk with God. I hope I will always be aware of God's presence guiding and moving me through the seasons of His ways."

I spent one of my hundred nights alone on the trail at Tagg Run Shelters. Of course, I was not totally alone. Mice inhabit most Appalachian Trial shelters.

"I came to the trail's current midpoint marker and rested a while to thank God for giving me the strength to make it that far."

I got a late start from Tagg Run but had a great cold-weather hike into Pine Grove Furnace State Park. There I came to the trail's current midpoint marker and rested a while to thank God for giving me the strength to make it that far. God had been faithful for 1,080 miles. I was often weary and wanted to quit, but His strength always lifted me. Knowing I still had a long way to travel, I thought about people I had heard or read of who left the trail after hiking more than a thousand miles. I prayed for renewed strength, perseverance and the ability to see the wonders of God's creation in a new way. The park, which takes its name from a Revolutionary War-era iron smelter, is located in a beautiful forest containing Fuller Lake. It was too cold to go swimming that day, and the Ironmaster's Mansion, now used as a youth hostel, was closed. However, a nice couple named John and Barbara, who were traveling cross country by RV, treated me to snacks and juice. On the other side of the park, the trail meandered up old roads and through the woods to Toms Run Shelters. I decided to hike an additional six and a half miles over South Mountain to Birch Run Shelters. I arrived at dark with the temperature 34 degrees and spent a peaceful night.

"It was beautifully silent this morning. I got up before dawn, prayed and ate breakfast wearing all my clothing in the 25-degree chill. There was a frost on the ground. It was a wonderful feeling, being out in the cold stillness of the wilderness. I hiked across the ridge and down to Caledonia State Park, passing Quarry Shelters and noting the many rhododendrons along the trail. Then I hiked over two miles of Pennsylvania rocks up to Rocky Mountain, intending to stay at new shelters on the ridge. I felt I could go on, however. I wanted to reach the town of South Mountain before the post office closed. I arrived there around 3 p.m. and received my new food package. There were also more onions from Madlyn and a ton of high-calorie cake from the Skinners. I bought some things at the general store and hiked the mile and a half out of town to the trail, continuing south about a quarter of a mile and setting up my tent under pine trees. On a thick bed of fallen needles I rested peacefully, as if sleeping on the best of mattresses. God has indeed supplied all my needs according to all His riches."

Just north of Pine Grove Furnace State Park is the unofficial half way mark sign. Although the trail is constantly in change, this symbolic sign was built by an Appalachian thru-hiker named "Woodchuck" in 1985.

I crossed this stream on a chilly morning in Warner Gap Hollow, Maryland. It reminded me of Psalm 42:1. "As the deer panteth for the water brooks, so panteth my soul after Thee, O God."

Night Hike over White Rocks

Maryland

I had no idea what time it was when I awoke at Birch Run, but it was cloudy as I left for the trail. I climbed over a rocky ridge to Snowy Mountain and the brand new Tumbling Run Shelters, then headed through a forest bursting with color. Passing by Antietam Shelter and Antietam Creek in the valley, I went over two more hills to Deer Lick Shelters and had lunch. In three more miles I arrived at Pen-Mar County Park on the Pennsylvania Maryland border. It was almost November now, and 1,110 miles had passed under my feet. Autumn seemed to be burning the countryside like a fire as I entered Maryland.

I pushed on to Quirauk Mountain, hiking a tremendously rocky trail that rose a thousand vertical feet. At the top of the ridge I took the side trail down to Devil's Racecourse Shelter – finding it, after all that effort, 500 vertical feet below the ridge and a half mile away. Also, the shelter was near a road, and I heard a dog barking all night. Staying in a shelter so named on Halloween night – with a full moon, no less – was spooky. As I lay wide awake listening to night sounds, I prayed that God would protect me and help me sleep.

"I don't know what time it is, but a strange thing just happened. Because of the full moon, I can see well outside the shelter. I was awakened by dogs going right by the shelter – first a beagle-type hound and then a type of shepherd. I saw a single bright light bobbing off in the distance, as if a person was carrying a lantern, but I couldn't see anyone. I was lying snugly in my sleeping bag, peering out into the darkness, and my heart started beating faster. Then, five minutes later, the dogs began barking very strangely. One started to yelp. The other howled. One is still yelping as I write this. The sounds keep getting closer and

I had to begin hiking at night because the days were getting shorter in November. In the late evening I sat upon White Rocks overlooking the Maryland countryside.

"Hiking in the wilder-ness at night with a full moon, and with the companionship of God, was a beautiful experience."

are coming from behind the shelter. I have prayed: 'God, You're my fortress and protector. I fear you, O Lord. You are the saving strength in whom I trust. You are my song and shield, the Rock of Ages, Creator and Lord of all creation.' Now I don't know what else to do."

I stayed in the shelter and hoped for the night to end soon. It was so strange seeing that lantern bob up and down in the distance, apparently with no one holding it. The dogs, although they moved away from the shelter, continued to bark in the distance. Maybe this was a coon hunt. I am not sure. All I can say is that it was an unusual night, and I could not wait for the morning light so I could get back on the trail. Early in the morning I hiked back up to the ridge and walked over South Mountain. Some rocky sections of the trail reminded me of Pennsylvania. As I passed by Pine Knob Shelter, I saw Rueven. He said he wanted to spend the Sabbath in the Harpers Ferry Campground with me. I left him after a short talk and hiked along the ridge, trying to get to Rocky Run Shelter before dark. On the way I passed a large stone structure with an observation deck, built in 1827 and called The Washington Monument. While gazing over the countryside, I talked with a bird-watcher who was looking for hawks. Once I arrived at Dahlgren Backpackers Camping Area, with its free hot showers (although mine was cold), I decided to hike to Crampton Gap Shelter. This would make my longest trail day, 26 miles including my first extended night hike. After showering, I cooked a rice dinner and left the camping area in the dark as the moon was rising.

"What a hike over Lambs Knoll! More than six and a half miles in the dark! It was so warm it seemed almost like a summer night. Hiking in the wilderness at night with a full moon, and with the companionship of God, was a beautiful experience. I sat for a long while on top of Lambs knoll, looking over the twinkling lights in the valley below White Rocks Overlook. The magnificent scene held me in a state of wonder at God's creation. God placed man on earth to dwell in union with Him and His creation. I praise Him for His faithfulness and for the love He has shown me. In this trail experience He has blessed me with many precious moments. Lord, help me not to waste them or let them fall to the ground. Help me see you clearly in them all."

After writing in the Crampton Gap Shelter register, I fell asleep – only to be awakened abruptly before dawn by Rueven. He had walked all night from Boonville, Maryland, and we were quite surprised to see each other. He soon left, in a hurry to get to Harpers Ferry. About an hour later I watched the sun rise, its amber rays filtering beautifully through trees. I then left the shelter and hiked into Gathland State Park. I met a day hiker named John, a wonderful Christian man who invited me to his home the following weekend when I would be in Harpers Ferry.

The trail descending Mt. Dunlop into Pen-Mar was ablaze with autumn color at the end of October.

Standing upon Jefferson's Rock and looking back towards Harpers Ferry.

West Virginia

Harpers Ferry Historical Park

West Virginia

From Crampton Gap I hiked the South Mountain ridge to a breathtaking overlook on Weverton Cliffs. After sitting a while and looking down on the mighty Potomac River, I hiked down the cliffs and walked three miles along the historic C&O Canal towpath. Then I crossed the Potomac on the 600-foot walkway that leads into Harpers Ferry National Historic Park. Eventually I came to the Appalachian Trail Conference Headquarters, where I was greeted by Jean Cashin, the wonderful woman with whom I had spoken by phone in preparing for my hike. It was a genuine pleasure to meet her. We talked for an hour.

"I made it to the post office by 3:30, picked up my mail, then headed over to the campground and cooked a huge spaghetti dinner. Rueven, with a tent site picked out already, met me. I am writing this by moonlight on the picnic table near my tent, enjoying the smell of nearby campfires and looking forward to a Sabbath rest."

The Appalachian Trail goes right through historic Harpers Ferry National Historic Park. Harpers Ferry is the home of the Appalachian Trail Conference.

John, the man I had met the previous day, came by in the morning, and we agreed to meet later for a walk near Harpers Ferry. I talked with Rueven most of the morning. When John returned with his wife Cheryl and a Russian girl named Alvena (who was studying theology at a school in Washington), we left Rueven and traveled to the C&O Canal. We hiked up the Grant Conway Trail to Maryland Heights, where we enjoyed marvelous views of the area. As the sun set over Harpers Ferry, we had a wonderful time of fellowship and prayer. John and Cheryl then took me out for dinner and returned me to the campground. After such a peaceful day I slept soundly.

The Appalachian Trail travels only about 17 miles through West Virginia, most of this segment following the Virginia-West Virginia border on Blue Ridge Mountain. In the two-mile walk back to town from the campground, I got lost and had to backtrack, but I found the trail again. I had breakfast near the ATC Headquarters and then climbed out of town along a small ridge to Jefferson Rock. There I photographed part of Harpers Ferry and the Shenandoah River, which joins the Potomac at that point. The trail then crosses the Shenandoah River Bridge and begins a 1,000-foot ascent of Loudoun Heights, an important outlook for Harpers Ferry during the Civil War.

I was exhausted when I reached Blackburn Trail Center two hours after dark, having hiked 10 miles across the high points of Blue Ridge Mountain. (Hiking was always difficult after leaving a trail town because my pack was at its heaviest.) The trail center was beautifully situated on the mountainside, its cabins for hikers fitted with screened-in porches, solar showers and wood stoves. As the only person there that night, I enjoyed peace and quiet. In the tranquillity of my cabin, I fell right to sleep.

I had planned an 18-mile hike to Rod Hollow Shelter the next day, but after a mile I did not want to hike any more. I was exhausted and felt defeated. It was definitely a low point in my journey. My spirit for hiking was no longer there. *"I wanted to give it all up today."* I decided to move on slowly, just to get to Bear's Den Hostel, which was seven miles ahead. A few miles down the trail I came to the top of a cliff called Crescent Rock and noticed a rope tied to a tree. Carefully craning my neck, I looked down and saw a couple preparing to climb the rock face. They called to me, asking if I wanted to climb with them. In no mood to take another step, I said "Sure!", took off my pack and walked down a side trail.

"God knows my frame and what is inside me. This is just what I need-ed to awaken the dead spirit within me. Rock-climbing! Using only my finger-tips and toes to climb straight up a rock wall! For more than five hours this after-noon, I learned rock climbing techniques from Doug and Jenny. On my first ascent I made it three fourths of the way up the cliff face, and on my last try, after some difficult moves, I made it to the top. Praise God! It was exhilarating — a blessing from God to have provided a much-needed mental break. The Lord is faithful and knows me so personally. This day, perhaps, would not have refreshed everyone's spirits, but it did mine. I hiked with a quicker step in the remaining miles to Bear's Den Hostel, covering the last half mile in pitch darkness. The place looked like a stone castle, a bit foreboding in the dark, but its caretakers, John and Jen, were extremely friendly. I was the only one staying there that night. I took a long shower, cooked dinner, settled into a bunk and fell fast asleep."

Ascending Crescent Cliffs with the help of a couple who were rock climbing.

Weverton Cliffs overlook the Potomac River near Harpers Ferry, WV.

141

An early morning fog covers the trees along Johns Creek Mountain in Virginia.

The Southern Appalachians

Virginia

Just after leaving Crescent Rocks I crossed into Virginia. This began my longest trek in any one state, for Virginia has more than 530 miles of trail. I started the day at Bear's Den Hostel by buying four eggs, scrambling them with scallions and eating them while drinking five glasses of milk. I was thankful for the previous day's rock-climbing opportunity, but my arms were so sore that I could hardly lift my pack. I left the hostel at mid-morning and hiked 10 miles through wooded hills to Rod Hollow Shelter. On the way I tripped over a rock and did a total flip in the air, landing on my back. That was the third time this happened to me, and thankfully my pack frame survived the impact. At Rod Hollow I was greeted by Phil, James and Andy, young men from Capitol Hill who had a large fire going. It was great to talk with them, and I prayed that God would touch their lives, guiding them in upcoming decisions. They were still asleep when I left the shelter in the morning and continued along the ridge into Sky Meadows State Park.

The trail went up and down many hills on the way to Linden, my next trail town. After hiking 16 miles to the road crossing, I thought I would not make it to the post office before it closed – even though it was no more than a mile from the trail. I did make it, and it took me more than an hour to get my new supplies organized. I then visited a country store and tried to get back to the trail as soon as possible, for it was getting dark. Two policemen I met at the store offered me a ride to the trail head. I hiked three miles by head lamp to Jim and Molly Denton Shelter, one of the best shelters on the Appalachian Trail. With its huge patio, cook-

Bob, Jamie and Canaan invited me to stay in the Pocosin Cabin on a 20- degree night.

ing pavilion and brick walkway, the place is like a palace. I did not want to leave it in the morning.

"The deer walked in graceful beauty and in gentleness toward me".

Chips and Salsa

After hiking a few miles the next day, I descended to Bear Hollow and Route 522. The trail passed by the National Zoological Park, then meandered up and down for a few miles before ascending steeply to the northern ridge line of Shenandoah National Park. At a registration station on the park boundary, I filled out a back country permit, not realizing I would be climbing to more than 3,350 feet in reaching the top of North Marshal Mountain, the trail's highest point since Mt. Greylock in Massachusetts.

"I can't believe how cold it is outside. The temperature never got out of the 30s today, and now it's down into the 20s. These last 18 miles to Gravel Springs Hut have been grueling — so many ups and downs, but mostly ups. I had to walk the last two and a half miles in the dark to make it to this quiet stone shelter. A deer passed by while I was cooking dinner. Now, as I write, there are huge rats — or rodents of some kind the size of small cats — crawling at the other end of the shelter. I can't believe the size of these things!!! Mice crawling on me or in my pack are one thing, but I wouldn't want one of these creatures to come anywhere near me. It is hard to tell what they are, maybe weasels or opossums. They look like huge ugly beasts compared to mice. I pray they don't crawl on me during the night."

It was another hard day for me as I hiked 13 miles over 3,474-foot Hogback Mountain. From there the trail went down and then up over Pass Mountain before coming to Pass Mountain Hut, where Rueven and Sondra were waiting for me with a beautiful roaring fire. We talked late into the night, and rain pelting the roof eventually soothed us to sleep. In the morning, a cold damp Sabbath, Sondra and I walked into Thornton Gap and ate at the Panorama Restaurant. We returned with chips and salsa sent with Sondra by my good friend Sam, who worked at a Chi-Chi's restaurant back home. In the afternoon I took a delightful nap and awoke to the sound of Rueven reciting another Devar Torah. He prayed until the sun set and stars appeared, at times screaming his petitions to God for deliverance from the frigid wind that permeated our open-air hut. I was thankful for the day's rest, good friendship and the new sleeping bag (rated to minus 5 degrees) that Sondra brought from home.

I left the shelter in early-morning chill and climbed to Mary's Rock and The Pinnacle at 3,730 feet. The trail then zigzagged up and down the ridge, following the Blue Ridge Parkway. The air was quite cold, especially on exposed overlooks. Autumn had definitely passed, for the trees were bare and the ground and trail were covered with decaying leaves. Seeing pieces of ice

Rueven (who was dressed in hunter orange so he would not be accidentally shot in the woods) and Sondra shared a Sabbath rest with me in Pass Mountain Hut.

along the way, I wondered how cold it would get as I walked farther south.

After hiking more than 10 miles, I passed by Stony Man Mountain and an area of Shenandoah Park called Skyland. Nearing Pollock Knob, I stopped to rest and snack on chips. While I sat there and munched, a lone white-tailed deer came over the ridge and stared at me. I kept eating but reached into my pack for my camera. Then, suddenly, two other deer came out of the woods and crept closer to me. I could not believe my eyes as the deer walked in graceful beauty and in gentleness toward me. There was a sweet cool stillness in the air as I sat quietly eating chips with the deer approaching. When they came to within six feet of me, I slowly raised a chip toward them. The deer closest to me timidly took one more step and ate the chip from my open hand. For an hour afterward my new friends and I shared this snack in the wilderness. I could actually touch their cold noses and feel their warm fur. As I sat there in the forest with three deer wandering all about me, I sensed God's loving Spirit. In the course of my journey I often sang a worship song that comes from one of the Psalms: "As the deer panteth for the water, so my soul longeth after Thee. You alone are my heart's desire, and I long to worship Thee..." It was a sad moment when I felt I needed to resume my hike and leave these beautiful creatures behind in the wilderness.

Fire Trucks

In the next eight miles I passed by many overlooks and went over Hawksbill Mountain and into Big Meadows. My lunch with the deer took a little longer than I realized because it was after dark when I met Sondra. We went to Skyland for dinner and did not get back to Big Meadows Lodge until 11 p.m. Reorganizing my gear took me into the wee hours, so I did not leave Big Meadows until mid-morning. After a huge breakfast in the lodge, I said good-bye to Sondra. The next 12 miles were hilly with the trail going over Hazeltop Mountain at 3,812 feet to a place near the summit of Bearfence Mountain where I planned to camp. Pocosin Cabin was normally locked, but I knew there was a good spring and privy nearby. When I arrived there just before sundown, I was met by a wonderful family from Maryland, Rob and Jamie and their daughter Canaan. They were having difficulty getting a fire going in the cabin's wood stove, so I volunteered to help. While I was at work, they invited me to use an empty bunk. On a 20-degree night I could hardly refuse. It was a privilege to sleep in warmth on a comfortable mattress. Awakening a number of times during the night to feed the stove, I heard the bone-chilling wind brush over the cabin and felt blessed.

View from Big Flat Mountain of Shenandoah National Park, Virginia. Virginia has the longest segment of the trail – more than 500 miles – of any of the 14 states through which it passes.

Blue Ridge Parkway at Stoney Man Mountain overlook.

Virginia

The Appalachian Trail heads into Shenandoah National Park and passes over
Compton Mountain.

Deer along the Appalachian Trail on Bushy Top Mountain. As I rested along the trail, deer came out of the woods, and for the next hour
we shared company and a snack.

I did not want to leave in the morning, but the trail was calling. I walked out of the cabin into frost and hiked 18 miles, the trail crossing the Blue Ridge Parkway six times. Within a few miles of the cabin I climbed 3,600-foot Baldface Mountain, then hiked down to Swift River Gap at 2,367 feet, and then in three miles was back up to Hightop Mountain at 3,587 feet. In the next eight miles the trail traversed smaller peaks and gaps on the way to Pinefield Hut. Meeting no one, I enjoyed a great peace with God, praising Him at times and at times walking in silence. That night it was close to freezing again, and I could hear the cascading stream near the cabin. The mice were busy, scuttling about me and my gear, and when I went outside in the middle of the night, I saw a doe standing there and staring at me.

I left in the morning when the sun was two fists above the horizon, noticing that the winding trails in this section of Shenandoah National Park were almost perfect for walking, with few rocks and roots. I hiked over many 3,000-foot peaks and came to Blackrock Hut, where I read the trail register, got water from the spring, and decided to do another night hike to make it to Calf Mountain Shelter.

"I am now sitting comfortably on a thick bed of pine needles in the middle of the Appalachian Trail. I just had to stop and enjoy this magnificent place. It is a crystal clear moonless night, and stars are twinkling to the horizon. There are pine trees lining the trail along the crest of the ridge, and a gentle breeze is blowing over the mountain. My heart is filled with peace. God's eternal presence has wrapped itself around me. I just saw a shooting star fly across the sky as my prayers of thanksgiving ascended to heaven. It has been a beautiful experience, walking the ridge at night. Lights were twinkling in the valleys on both sides of the narrow ridge. It is gorgeous. And now I feel the quietness of the night. An animal just screeched out a sound that I never heard before."

The last few miles of that night hike were outside the park, and the trail immediately became rocky, root-filled and uneven again. I woke two hikers in the shelter when I came sauntering in like a miner with my head lamp on after 10 p.m. Brad and Rich (The Hoosiers) had been hiking the Appalachian Trial in sections for 16 years. We talked for about an hour while I ate dinner. It had been a great day – 27 miles.

The three of us left the shelter in the early morning. Brad and Rich hiked with me for a few miles and took a side trail while I continued south, reaching 1,902-foot Rockfish Gap near the southern entrance to Shenandoah Park. There Route 250 crosses the ridge and goes down into Waynesboro, my next trail town. I was trying to get into town early enough in the day to pick up my mail, organize and get back to the trail before dark. I could not believe it, but in three miles of downhill walking on that busy road not a single person picked me up. Near the bottom of the hill an old gen-

tleman named Zach (a funeral director) graciously offered me a ride to the fire station where thru-hikers were allowed to stay, but I declined the ride. Instead, I walked to an outdoor equipment store and bought a few items. Then I hobbled to the fire station, where a firefighter named Charles showed me around and said I could sleep on the floor near the trucks. No other hiker had been through in a while, and I had the whole place to myself. I eased the pack off my back, took a shower and then went to the post office and a laundromat. I also visited a grocery store and bought a whole cooked chicken and cole slaw, which I gobbled down with a half gallon of orange juice. *"It is hard to imagine being on a wilderness adventure and now lying on the floor of a fire station with five shiny red trucks beside me. I thank God for His provision and shelter. I can hear the radio dispatcher calling out every few minutes."*

Hard Time Hollow

Thank God no fire alarms went off during the night. I was up early in the morning, packed and ready to be picked up by another old gentleman, Sam, who was going to drive me the five miles back up to Rockfish Gap. I got up to the gap and headed south again with more than 70 pounds on my back. On the first five miles up 2,700-foot Dobie Mountain I struggled, not knowing if I would have the energy and strength to climb Humpback Mountain at 3,600 feet. When I finally arrived at the Humpback summit, I was exhausted. I met two brothers, Tom and Frank, and for an hour we talked about walking with God. This boosted my spirit, and I felt refreshed as I continued down the trail. Once I got to Dripping Rock parking area on the Blue Ridge Highway, it was near the end of the day. I decided to walk along the parkway to get to a place called Rusty's Hard Time Hollow before sundown. Within a few minutes a couple of guys from Florida stopped their jeep and offered me a ride.

Hard Time Hollow is a small working farm with no running water or electricity, and the property is surrounded by park land. When I walked down the gated driveway from the parkway, I saw Rueven. Also to my surprise, I saw Andy, Rich and Brandon (Pigpen, Speed and The Beastmaster) from Ohio. I could not believe those guys were there. From reading shelter registers I had surmised that they were about three weeks ahead of me, but when they had arrived at Rusty's, it was getting cold and they decided to leave the trail and stay.

Rusty, a fascinating person, had lived 11 years among Mennonites and had been at Hard Time Hollow since 1979. When

"It was awesome to walk down the mountainside with the feeling of swimming in the leaves."

he found out that Appalachian Trail hikers came within a few miles of his home, he thought it would be great to provide them with a place for shelter, friendship and rest. People stayed at the farm for a day, a week, or sometimes more than a month. Rusty showed me around, and we talked for hours.

Meanwhile, Rueven, who was staying in a small camper next to the house and setting up for the Sabbath, nearly burned the place down. He had put his candles on the white shirt he used as a table-cloth and then lighted them. While praying, though, he fell asleep, and the candles caught the shirt and a Formica-topped table on fire. When I walked into the trailer, smoke was pouring out. I gasped for breath, not knowing how Rueven could be alive inside. Fortunately, he was all right, and the only damage done was to the shirt and table – and there was the lingering odor of smoke, of course. Rusty found Rueven an intriguing character and tried to record the songs and prayers he chanted.

Later that day a 1989 thru-hiker from Atlanta came by with a bucket of fried chicken that we feasted on around the wood-burning stove in Rusty's house. We talked until late in the evening as the temperature fell. It was great to run into Andy, Rich and Brandon again. I had not seen them since we stayed at the Catholic hostel in Cheshire, Massachusetts. The next day I took a short walk on the trail with Rich, and we talked about what he was going to do in the future. People came and went at the farm all day. I decided to take an extra day off to help Rusty by cleaning the grounds and the house. A northbound thru-hiker named Cruise Control came by. He had just finished his Appalachian Trail journey by completing a short section he missed on the way north. At about 10 p.m. a number of us enjoyed a warm soak in Rusty's hot tub, which was near his potato field about a hundred yards from the house. It was 28 degrees out, and stars were twinkling in the sky.

The next morning Andy and I left the hollow early to hike another section of the trail. We began near Maupin Field Shelter at Reeds Gap and climbed Three Ridges, came down to the Tye River, then worked our way up again to the 4,063-foot summit of The Priest. The trail wound along a ridge line for the next six miles and ascended Maintop Mountain at 4,040 feet. Fallen leaves were piled so deep in places that they were almost up to our waist. It was awesome to walk down the mountainside with the feeling of swimming in the leaves – although there was the danger of twisting an ankle because we could not see rocks or roots in the trail. For the last two miles of this 20-mile day we hiked in the dark, then waited in frigid air for Rusty to pick us up on Fish Hatchery Road. Exhausted, I decided to stay at the hollow one more day and work. The place was so comfortable that some hikers never get back to the trail once they arrive. I was beginning to see why.

Rusty with Pigpen, Speed and The Beastmaster, who had
been at the hollow for over a week.

Many thru-hikers visit Rusty's Hard Time Hollow, which is surrounded by park land.

Hunters and Donkeys

"There was a cool blue sky overhead as I hiked south, seeing many hunters."

In the morning I said good-bye to Andy, Rich and Brandon, whose grandfather had come to take them back to Ohio. Three hunters in a pickup took me back up to the trail head. As we traveled up a bumpy dirt road, we stopped to pick up a skinny old mountain man. Clad in dirty overalls, he was carrying two bags, one with groceries and the other containing fuel in a one-gallon plastic bottle. He told us he was walking to his home in the woods, and as he smiled his wrinkly grin revealed no teeth. When the two of us were dropped off at the Appalachian Trail junction, I had no idea where he was going. There was no dwelling within a mile of the ridge line where we were standing. He told me he lived, along with his mother and brothers, in a log cabin on 300 acres more than a mile away on the other side of the next mountain. The family had lived there for more than 50 years. Since there was no road into the place, they carried all their goods to the house on foot.

There was a cool blue sky overhead as I hiked south, seeing many hunters. I was a bit nervous, for I had read recently in a shelter register that a southbounder quit his hike after a bullet whizzed by his head near a trail junction. While taking pictures of a beautiful pattern in rocks and trees on Porters Ridge, I suddenly heard a man call to me. Sitting camouflaged on a high rock about 50 yards away, he had been watching me for 15 minutes or so. He said I should be making more noise along the trail because a hunter could easily mistake me for a deer. Learning that I had no bright orange clothing, this fine Virginia gentleman gave me his lightweight orange vest and suggested that I drape it over my pack. After talking for a while we prayed together, and I continued hiking. I went over bald mountains on Tar Jacket Ridge, then came to a small camp where two slain deer were hanging on a tree limb. Down in Hog Camp Gap I met another hunter who, with his friends, had shot 14 deer that season and had 500 pounds of venison stored in the family freezer. This man felt I still did not have enough bright orange clothing on, so he gave me an orange day-glow cap. He was afraid I might get shot at going up the trail, being mistaken for a deer. It had never occurred to me that the Appalachian Trail was so commonly used for hunting. Continuing up the ridge, I came to the bald top of 4,022-foot Cole Mountain and the wooded summit of Bald Knob at 4,059 feet. The trail then descended three miles to Route 60, where Rusty was waiting to pick me up for my last night at the hollow.

The next morning Wilderness Bob drove me back to the trail, and I followed it into the lower mountains bordering Lynchburg Reservoir. While photographing ferns I met Joseph, an older gentleman who said he often hiked this section of trail, his wife dropping him off at one road crossing and picking him up at

Virginia

This hunter in Hog Camp Gap gave me an orange cap so I would not get shot going up the trail.

A very stubborn donkey on the farm prevented me from hiking down the trail.

The Appalachian Trail goes through this farm near the Lynchburg Dam in Virginia.

"Then the donkey suddenly lunged and with no hesitation began biting my shirt and skin – even my pack."

another. We talked of our love for God and the wilderness. It was a joy to meet wonderfully kind people such as him and others I came upon in this wilderness corridor. After rounding the lake's rugged shore, the trail crossed in front of a large dam on a footbridge over Little Irish Creek. Soon after coming to a narrow dirt road lined by barbed wire fence, I saw donkeys approaching. As I neared the one in the lead, it looked at me in a funny way and stopped, giving no appearance that it was likely to move out of the way when I walked by. I talked nicely, inching forward. Then the donkey suddenly lunged and with no hesitation began biting my shirt and skin – even my pack. I backed off quickly, not knowing what to do and feeling nervous and trapped by both the animal and the fences. I tried again to get by, but every time I approached, no matter how sweetly I talked, the donkey kept nipping at me. At last, after 15 minutes or so, I used my staff to defend myself. I carefully kept it between me and the donkey as I slowly skirted its right side. It took a step or two toward me, but I stretched past its hind quarters. As I did so, I thought it would either kick me or turn and come after me, but it did neither. I still had to pass its friends, which had stopped and watched the drama without interest. After passing by them, I felt relieved and began to wonder what purpose God had in all this – knowing that all aspects of time, including delays, are in His hands.

Eyes in the Night

The trail ascended 2,208-foot Rice Mountain through bare forests, then in two miles crossed the Blue Ridge Parkway to Punchbowl Shelter. When I arrived there around sunset, I met a woman named Elaine. It was the eve of Thanksgiving, and her daughter had gone to New York for the holiday, so she had come onto the trail. As I prepared soup for dinner, Elaine pulled two huge turkey legs out of her pack and gave me one. I shared my soup, and we enjoyed a holiday feast in the wilderness. I then went on because I was going to be picked up at the James River crossing the day after Thanksgiving by Bill and Mae Green of Danville. My friend Michael and I had lived with these people in California for five months while on a cross-country trip after graduating from college. The James River was more than 10 miles away. So I entered the Appalachian wilderness again in complete darkness, beginning a nine-mile trek up 3,372-foot Bluff Mountain. There were many bumps and sags along the ridge and a climb of Big Rocky Row before I came down steeply to the river.

While sitting in a cold stiff wind on the Bluff Mountain Overlook, I heard a loud rustling off in the woods. I had heard similar sounds earlier in ascending the mountain. As I turned my head lamp in the direction of the sound, my heart leaped, for at least

three pairs of bright eyes were staring at me out of the dark woods. I could not tell what kind of animals they were, but I knew they had been following me for quite a while on that ridge. At times, it was pretty spooky. I would stop and shine my light into the forest and see a pair of eyes fixed on me. At times they just stared at me and then disappeared quickly into the darkness. Closer to the river the trail descended steeply to Fullers Rocks, then continued down a slippery rock slide. I could not believe, after walking for hours on the ridge, that I was stumbling down a rock slide by head lamp. It must have been past midnight when I reached Johns Hollow Shelter, two miles beyond the slide. I was glad no one was there because I would surely have scared them coming in so late. I praised God for giving me strength and keeping me safe.

The next morning I awoke as the sun came up. I ate break-fast quickly, packed up and headed for the river. Within an hour Mae and her son Richie picked me up, and we traveled to Danville, where I helped set up for Richie's wedding. The following day, a time of happy celebration and fellowship with the family, made a great Sabbath. *"I went to church with Mae and Bill. After a filling meal at Shoney's we all scrunched, along with my backpack, into Bill's Porsche. We headed back to the James River, where they dropped me off, well fed and toting a much heavier pack. I hiked only two and a half miles before dark and stayed the night at Matt's Creek Shelter. All night long I heard the creek playing a wonder-ful symphony, a myriad of floating voices and music. God, may your Holy Spirit fill me with joy, laughter and happiness — just as this stream flows contin-uously and fills the earth with its timeless sound."*

I left the shelter shortly after dawn and climbed more than 10 miles to 4,137-foot Apple Orchard Mountain, the highest point I had come to since Mt. Killington in Vermont. The trail crossed the parkway twice, then followed the Thunder Ridge Wilderness. It was an exceptionally warm day – 60 degrees. After hiking 17 miles I rejoiced in making it into Cornelius Creek Shelter before dark. I hardly slept a wink, though, because the shelter had a major mouse problem. About a dozen mice were running all over the place all night long!

The next day was also gorgeous, and I had rough terrain to cover. The first five miles into Bryant Gap, after coming off of Floyd Mountain, were not difficult. But then the trail rose 1,700 vertical feet over 10 knobs in ascending Fork Mountain on the way to the summit of Cove Mountain. Once on the ridge line, the trail followed the parkway to Bobblets Gap Shelter where I spent the night. At the break of dawn the following day, I hiked five miles of trail that parallel and cross the parkway. I waited at Taylors Mountain Overlook for Jeff (The Lummox) from Ohio, who was coming to visit me. When he arrived, we reminisced about our hik-ing in Maine, and I drank a whole bottle of cranberry juice cocktail that he gave me. We decided that I should continue south while he drove around to a road crossing near Troutville and hiked north to

The towns of Cloverdale and Troutville can be seen in the valley from Tinker Ridge.

"Nature truly has her own gentle rhythm."

meet me. In five hours we met again and rested near the 2,676-foot summit of Fulhardt Knob. We then came down more than a thousand vertical feet into the valley where the trail goes through Troutville.

"*It was great hiking with Jeff again after not seeing him for more than four months. The eight miles to Fulhardt Knob were very hard, filled with many ups and downs. It was so warm today that for the first time since Vermont I was completely soaked with sweat. It ran down my legs, soaking my socks and boots. I was drenched. Jeff and I went to the post office, where I received a Thanksgiving package from Sondra and chips and salsa from Steve and Lisa. God bless them. At the Knights Inn I took a super-long shower and did laundry. After an all-you-can-eat dinner at Western Sizzler I was so stuffed that I could hardly move. For more than an hour I talked with Mike, a cousin of Steve (The Great White Bowana). Having helped Steve on his thru-hike, Mike was planning to meet Jeff and me for breakfast the following morning.*"

Peace Walk

The next day was glorious. Mike treated Jeff and me to a huge breakfast at Shoney's, and we had a great time talking about life and our journeys with God. I got everything together by 10 a.m., then Jeff took me to Route 652 above Troutville, where I began a three-mile walk down into the town, passing by the Western Sizzler. At an Exxon station where the trail headed off the road into the woods, I stopped for a last taste of civilization: two hot dogs, a Danish and two bottles of orange juice. It was difficult to shoulder my 70-pound pack and leave the comforts of the valley. As I walked down the trail into the fresh-smelling forest, away from the hustle and bustle of society, I felt instantly transformed and at peace. The noise from the city and the highways faded slowly into the quietness permeating God's natural creation. I hiked a steep trail to Tinker Mountain and had great views of towns below and Carvin Cove Reservoir on the other side of the mountain.

At one point along the ridge I was filled with such joy that I had to stop and write. "*Nature truly has her own gentle rhythm. After walking through Troutville under Interstate 81, I sat down and watched people rushing about, their trucks, jeeps, and cars speeding along the highways. Restaurants, TVs, motels and the hustle and bustle of everyday life created a noisy whirlwind, and nobody seemed to notice it. And yet within five minutes of taking the trail down into the wilderness, I could hear, see and feel God's creation — moving at its own pace, in its own time, in a beauty and quietness that was His alone. The earth, the dark soil so still and unmoving, and the leaves ever melting into the ground while giving new life — so much is happening all around me, yet there is a true deep peace here. For most of us this feeling is accessible, sometimes just a stone's throw from the world that spins furiously around us, but intimacy with God and His creation takes time. Thus, if only occasionally, we need to step*

off the world's treadmill for a walk in the wilderness. We need to linger on the path of peace."

The ridge trail led over many little peaks and overlooks, and at dusk, after hiking 11 miles, I stopped for an early dinner at Lamberts Meadows Shelter. The night was chilly but cloudless, so I decided to walk over Tinker Cliffs and the beautiful McAfee Knob. It was a special moment when the full moon came out, silhouetting leafless trees on the ridges and illuminating the trail so I needed no lamp. I walked eight miles along the cliffs and ridges and stood on the knob, gazing at lights in the valley and the millions of twinkling stars that filled the heavens. It was an awe-inspiring sight. I then walked down to Catawba Mountain Shelter, where I spent my coldest night so far. A nylon liner prevented moisture from passing into the fill of my down sleeping bag. I was warmer than I would have been otherwise, but I felt a bit claustrophobic inside the liner. Awakening to temperatures in the teens and frozen water bottles, I quickly packed and started moving. But the previous day's 24 miles had done me in. I was exhausted after just three miles. The high trails in this part of the Appalachians are like roller coaster tracks, presenting a stiff physical challenge.

As I sat on top of Catawba Mountain, I heard lots of gun fire. It was definitely the last day for many deer. Then, in coming down the mountain near Sandstone Ridge and walking across an open field, I saw an unusual sight. Rueven was walking toward me dressed from head to toe in hunter-orange clothing. Even the cows in the field were staring at him in all his fancy hiking regalia. Rueven thought I was going to be at Catawba Mountain Shelter for the Sabbath, but he was incorrect. I was headed for Pickle Branch Shelter, more than seven miles down the trail. As we stood in the middle of the pasture talking, Rueven glanced at his maps and decided that he could not make it to Pickle Branch by sundown if he remained on the trail. So he went down to hitch a ride to Route 620, which crosses the trail a mile north of the shelter, and I began climbing the jagged 3,050-foot Dragon's Tooth. With its 1,500 feet of elevation gain in two miles, this stretch of trail reminded me of Maine. I stumbled into the shelter exhausted just at dusk and saw that it was lighted by many Sabbath candles. Rueven, with his new trail name Roadwalker, had become adept at hitching rides on country roads. I quickly lit my own candles, cooked dinner and settled into the warmth of my sleeping bag for another very cold night.

It was a beautiful Sabbath. I slept until 10:30 and just sat around the shelter and walked through the surrounding forest, praying and enjoying God's wonderful presence all day. That night Rueven again yelled at the cold, saying this was going to be it for him on the trail. He never carried a sleeping bag. Instead, he wore ten or more layers of clothing at night to keep warm. With all that

"with its wonderful display of rhododendron and mountain laurel, it reminded me of Hawaii."

on he looked like a huge Pillsbury Dough Boy. When I left Rueven and Pickle Branch Shelter around 9:30 the next morning, there was a sprinkle in the air. I had a great hike over Branch Mountain, a new trail relocation. The trail then went down into a wooded valley, and after hiking 10 miles I stopped at Niday Shelter. It was so beautiful and quiet there that I had a hard time deciding whether to stay or go on. I still had a lot of energy, but Sarver Cabin, six miles distant, was supposedly not as nice as this spot.

I moved on, heading up Sinking Creek Mountain – a steep and rocky two miles – and then the trail crossed over cliffs and ledges for four more miles. When I got to the side trail that led to the steep descent to the cabin, I had second thoughts. It was rumored that the cabin was run down, and in hiking the ridge I had heard gun shots in the lowland. I decided to press on, pushing hard as night came to reach the Level Green Christian Church, where hikers could stay in a pavilion on the grounds. I walked the last five to six miles in the dark. Arriving so late, I was unsure if the pastor would let me stay. Hiking through fields into the valley had been frustrating. I got lost many times and had to work my way along barbed wire fences in the dark to find outlets for the trail. Pastor Jack let me use his house water because the tap at the pavilion was turned off. I had a fitful rest on the cement floor with a few mice visiting during the night.

Bears at Bay

The farm area I walked through this morning was beautiful! It began to rain as I hiked out of the valley toward Laurel Creek Shelter on the side of Johns Creek Mountain. The location of this shelter is magnificent. With its wonderful display of rhododendron and mountain laurel, it reminded me of Hawaii. Alex, the first hiker I had met in a long while, had done the trail in 1980 and went by the name Caper. We talked longer than an hour. (Being alone so much of the time, I usually ramble on whenever I meet someone.) After leaving Alex in increasingly heavy wind and rain, I hiked over Johns Creek Mountain and up here to War Spur Shelter. Having gone only eight and a half miles, I wanted to make the next shelter, which is seven miles away, but it was cold and wet. I knew that with the 2,000-foot vertical climb involved I would never make it there before dark. So I stayed here. I sat in my sleeping bag most of the late afternoon, drinking hot soup and listening to rain hitting the tin roof. Now, just before going to sleep, I feel I need to write about one more thing — a strange phenomenon. A while ago the rain stopped and then, within an hour, I began to feel a surprising warmth in the shelter. The temperature, which had dropped to the high 30s, is now almost 50 degrees. This is very unusual."

The next morning on my way up 4,128-foot Potts Mountain, I met a bear hunter whose four tick hounds were tied to a tree. He told me he was hunting with friends who were on the next mountain. They had spread out with their hounds trying to

Rueven on Sandstone Ridge, searching his maps for the closest way to the next shelter.

This hunter on Potts Mountain, along with his four tick hounds, awaits a call from friends and other hounds looking for bear.

find a bear's den. If their dogs found a bear in a den, they would start chasing the bear and contact this man by walkie-talkie. If it came in his direction, he would let his dogs go and join the chase. The bear could then be trapped and killed with a pistol. He was a nice guy, but I felt sad for any animal that would die in this way. The hike to the ridge was rocky and steep, and I walked mostly in clouds for the seven miles to Bailey Gap Shelter. When I got off the ridge, the wind died down, and the air "warmed" to 25 degrees. My water bottles were iced, and my feet were cold most of the day. I continued down Big Mountain into Stony Creek Valley, the trail surrounded by huge patches of mountain laurel and rhododendron as it meandered through the valley to Pine Swamp Shelter.

The wind picked up again, even in the valley. Extremely cold after being outside all day, I set out my sleeping bag quickly, got water and went to the outhouse. I then nestled my boots in the bottom of my sleeping bag. I also slept with a water bottle so I would have drinking water, not ice, in the morning. I was sitting in the bag, leaning against a shelter wall and eating my favorite trail meal, Sloppy Joe soup, when a mouse walked along the deck. According to the register, no one had visited this shelter in more than a month. In June a northbounder named The Grim Squeaker had caught and killed 10 mice there, which he stated was his new record. In the past few months I had little or no company at night except for these little fellows, and although they kept me up some nights, I enjoyed them. It was so cold that I felt sorry for this creature, so I put out a spoonful of my precious soup. For the next hour we shared a great dinner.

"Last night was the coldest for me on the trail so far. The temperature rarely got above the low 20s during the day. Most of the time it was in the teens, with the wind blowing 20 to 30 m.p.h. on the ridge tops. It snowed most of the day, but there was not a deep accumulation. Still, my toes were freezing because my boots were wet from rain the day before. Thankfully, this morning there is only a dusting of snow on the ground and my sleeping bag. In the early dawn I heated water for hot chocolate and cooked some oatmeal. Of course, I fed my little mice friends again, thinking that would probably be their last good meal for a while."

I left Pine Swamp Shelter just after light because I was chilled to the bone, even in my sleeping bag, which was losing loft because my body moisture was passing into the down. I quickly climbed a thousand vertical feet in a mile to reach the Peters Mountain ridge crest at 3,740 feet. A fiery cold blast of northwest wind hit me. The temperature had plummeted to below 10 degrees, and the wind was gusting at around 40 m.p.h. I had never experienced such cold. I was wearing all my clothing, and I was definitely not prepared for this. The freezing wind blew through my thin Gortex outer layer and my four layers of polypropylene. It was a 12-mile hike along the ridge, and the temperatures never

Snow and wind whirled around Pine Swamp Shelter all night long.

The winds blew more than 40 m.p.h., and the temperature was below 10 degrees on Peters Mountain.

163

moved above the teens until later in the day. I had to keep moving quickly just to keep warm in the brisk wind. I made it off Peters Mountain just before dark and began a very hilly section of the trail along Hemlock Ridge. The trail followed a ridge around a factory, then came to a bridge across the New River. There were many ups and downs, especially at the end of this long freezing day's hike. As I began the road walk into Pearisburg, I saw the bright signs of a Hardee's Restaurant half a mile away. This started my mouth watering. Fortunately, for I had no food left, I made it into town just in time for dinner. After a filling meal I walked two more miles to reach the Holy Family Church hostel. Church members had reconstructed an old barn for hikers to stay in, and there was a wood-burning stove in it but no water or shower in the winter. Finding no wood in the barn, I searched for about an hour for enough to heat the stove and take away the 20-degree nip in the air.

I decided to stay at a motel the next day so I could take a warm shower, do laundry, organize my mail and shop for food. By the time I finished all my errands, it was late afternoon. Because I had run out of food, I bought more than I needed, and my pack weighed close to 80 pounds again. Ouch! I wrote letters until 2 a.m. and woke around 9 o-clock to head back on the trail.

The 1,500-foot vertical climb to Angel's Rest at 3,350 feet on Pearis Mountain was difficult. I took my time, not wanting to sweat too much because of the frigid temperatures. The hike along the ridge went through thickets of rhododendron so dense that the trail was like a tunnel in places.

When I arrived at Doc's Knob Shelter, I gathered water and wood for a fire and settled in for two nights because the next day was the Sabbath. An hour later hikers Nate and Wendall showed up and made a huge fire. It was great, at last, to have someone to share a shelter with other than a few mice. During the next few hours by the fire's warmth we talked about life and the trail and prayed for one another. They even shared a delicious piece of steak, cooked with onions, peppers and tomatoes in tin-foil over the fire. Boy, was it delicious! I had prayed for some companionship during this Sabbath, and God brought me a double portion.

Vermin

In the morning Nate and Wendall wanted me to hike with them to the next shelter, but I told them I was taking a Sabbath rest. We prayed again before they left, knowing we would meet again. I rested in my sleeping bag most of the day since it was the warmest place when I was not hiking. Even so, I was pretty cold most of the day. The down in my bag was still losing loft, and without the sun it was hard to dry it out. In Pearisburg I had to

call my father to order a down jacket because I was getting too cold, especially when I stopped hiking at the end of the day. In the afternoon another hiker, Peter, arrived, and he made a big fire. We talked until after dark with the temperature in the low 20s again. I inadvertently left my water bottle on the shelter deck, and by morning it was frozen solid.

From the shelter the trail ascended 3,950-foot Doc's Knob and continued onto the high ridges of Flat Top Mountain and Sugar Run Mountain. After 10 miles of hiking in more comfortable 40-degree weather, I descended along beautiful Dismal Creek to Wapiti Shelter. I had lunch in the shelter and continued along the creek for about seven miles. I was rushing a bit to get to Jenny Knob Shelter (seven miles away) when I came to the trail's junction with the Dismal Creek Falls trail. On the sign was a note for me from Nate and Wendall saying there was a great place to camp near the falls. I did not know if I should rush on or enjoy the falls. After praying I decided to stay by the falls. Since the sun was only an hour from setting, I would never have made it to the next shelter before dark. I set up my tent on the rocks alongside the creek just below the falls and cooked a delicious spaghetti dinner. When I had almost finished it, I left to use the woods "rest room."

Returning, I heard my cooking pot clink and saw something move near it. I then watched in amazement as a huge rat nearly tipped over the pot. The animal was about to stick its face into my spaghetti when I ran toward it, but as it ran off, I saw that it was too late to save my dinner. I buried the remainder of the spaghetti. After cleaning the pot and getting ready to crawl into my tent, I noticed a pickup on an old dirt road on the other side of the stream. A strange looking man stepped out, stared at me a while, then mysteriously left. Considering the rat and the mystery man, I prayed earnestly for protection that night. Even as I slept, I was awakened by the rat again, or by another one. At any rate, an animal of some kind knocked over the cook pot during the night and actually tried to crawl over my tent. From inside I slapped the animal off. *"It was so cold overnight that by morning my tent was covered with frost inside and out. It was as if a snowstorm had hit inside my tent. My pack outside was also covered with heavy frost. I did not really have a great night's sleep."*

Cows

I woke early and hiked over the wooded crest of Brushy Mountain at 2,460 feet, then continued along a dirt road to Lickskillet Hollow. After one mile up Brushy Mountain again, the trail passed by Jenny Knob Shelter, where I stopped to have lunch. To reach the side trail to Helvey's Mill Shelter, I continued on the Bushy Mountain ridge for 10 miles. The shelter was about three tenths of a mile off the trail. Within another two and a half

Burkes Garden, sometimes called "God's Thumbprint," is a beautiful, fertile valley surrounded by mountains.

Rhododendron surround the trail often in the South and particularly in this section near Doc's Knob Shelter.

For many miles the Appalachian Trail follows and crosses Little Wolf Creek, which can be extremely dangerous in high water.

miles the trail would cross a road leading down to the town of Bastian, where a man named Levi Long had a hostel and diner. Passing up the shelter, I hiked down to Kimberlin Creek. A bath tub sitting in the water was supposed to have sodas in it, but unfortunately this was not the time of year for that. Once I reached the road that crossed the ridge, I came to a steep hill descending two miles to Bastian.

After hiking more than 20 miles, I was hoping someone would pick me up, but no one did. Finally, nearing the bottom of the hill after dark, I noticed that Jay Fred's Market was still open. I was starving and cold, so I left my pack outside the store and wandered in. Jay Fred was standing behind the counter talking with local folk. In a few minutes we discovered our common faith in Jesus, and the sweet fellowship we enjoyed from that point lasted two hours. While we were talking, Jay Fred kept feeding me turkey sandwiches and soda, and I tried to pay for them, but he refused. Eventually, he closed the store and drove me over to Levi's hostel, which was downstairs in "Mama Kate's" house across from the diner. It was quite rustic and a little damp inside, and I watched *The Wizard of Oz* on an old black and white TV.

After waking late I went to the diner for a hefty breakfast and listened to stories being told by old-timers. I left there to say good-bye to Jay Fred, who had two more sandwiches prepared for me to take on the trail. Having invited me to his church later in the week, he said he would pick me up at a place called Burkes Garden. I got a ride back up to the ridge from a fascinating old-timer, Luke, who had worked as a farmer, a saw mill hand and a surveyor. On the ridge top I was invited into the local senior center for coffee and ended up giving a half-hour talk. I finally got onto the trail around noon and followed the Brushy Mountain ridge six miles. For three miles the trail paralleled Little Wolf Creek, crossing it a dozen times. Rhododendron thickets made this section of trail magnificent. The trail then descended into the small valley where Hunting Camp Creek runs past Jenkins Shelter. This shelter is located between two mountains, and all night I could hear screech owls calling to one another. It was exciting yet eerie in the seclusion of that valley. Alone at the shelter, I read in the register about a storm the previous year that dumped more than a foot of snow in this valley. Three-foot drifts had made the trail impassable for some time.

In the morning I ascended Garden Mountain for three miles, reaching the 4,000-foot crest and following the ridge for six miles down to Walker Gap. All along this section of trail were great views of the beautiful Burkes Garden, a pristine valley nicknamed "God's Thumbprint." Once at Walker Gap, I walked down into this valley to the Burkes Garden post office. As I walked along, cows followed me along a fence for more than a mile. I waited only a little while for Jay Fred to arrive and take me to Bastian. We took many country roads and saw beautiful scenery. Arriving at Jay

Virginia

Burkes Garden from the valley floor.

Fred's house, I was greeted by his wife Peggy, who treated me just like one of her family. We had a super dinner, then went to church, where I spoke about the journey, my faith in God and walking with Jesus. Then we returned to the house and talked till midnight.

"Jay Fred woke me up around 6 a.m. and made me five fried eggs, six pieces of toast, hot dogs and potatoes. Then we made the hour drive back to Burkes Garden, and I started hiking up to Chestnut Knob at a high elevation of 4,409 feet. It was clouded in and quite cold. Chestnut Knob Shelter, called "Rocky" or "The Cave," sits atop the grassy summit. It was unoccupied and quite dark and dank. The hike down Chestnut Ridge was magnificent. It was grassy in places, and I could see all the mountains to the east and west. It was so beautiful and peaceful today. The trail came down into Poor Valley, where beavers have cut down many trees near Lick Creek. The rain came down heavily as I hiked up Lynn Camp Mountain to Knot Mole Shelter. I did not see anyone today and could not hear anything on this side of the mountain. It is truly an awesome wilderness place. I felt that God was close as the clouds came in and the wind picked up. It was only about 40 degrees, but that felt warm to me. It felt like summer in that every night the past few weeks had been below freezing. I love you, Lord, with all my heart, soul and strength."

After descending Brushy Mountain in the morning, the trail traveled along picturesque country roads and through wonderful farmland. I was surrounded by cows, horses, dogs, houses, people, and fields for more than two miles. I then left the valley and climbed Big Walker Mountain. *"I love the valleys, which are so full of life, but I love the mountains and ridges as well. I can sense God's awesome presence here. As I sat a few hundred feet below the Walker summit, I could hear the wind gusting on the other side of the mountain, yet I was in peaceful quiet. All I could hear nearby was the creaking of a slowly swaying tree. Nature seems to be so silent this time of year. You can truly hear the voice of God in this breathtaking silence. I need to bathe in it and take it all in — let God's Spirit fill my heart and mind with His peace."*

I met a man named Arten whose land was being used for the Appalachian Trail, which passed right next to his house. We talked for a bit while he was cutting down a tree, and he told me about the mixed feelings he had with the trail so close to his farm. After ascending Big Walker Mountain the trail went down into Crawfish Valley, another magnificently pristine area. I then ascended Gullion Mountain at 3,000 feet and descended through miles of pasture land into Davis Hollow, crossing many stiles in each field. The Appalachian Trail crosses many fields on its way from Maine to Georgia. Many of these are surrounded by barbed wire fences three to six feet high. Stiles — triangular ladders placed over fences — can be difficult to negotiate carrying a full pack. In a few of the fields I crossed in this area, there were many cows, and some of them walked a long way just to check me out. Others actually walked with me for a while. It was great to have the company as I hiked on these bleak wintry days.

The Burkes Garden Post Office.

The trail along Chestnut Knob leads to an old stone shelter at 4,410 feet.

The Appalachian Trail descends into the farm land of Ceres, VA.

After walking under Interstate 81 on the way to Atkins, I checked into a motel right next to the Appalachian Trail. The receptionist was gracious enough to give me a ride into town. When I came back, I gorged myself on fried chicken at the Village Inn restaurant, and the next day, a Sabbath, I just took it easy. I ate breakfast, lunch, and dinner at the restaurant and had a relaxing time just praying and getting my things together. I left in the morning after having one more home cooked meal and headed up the trail for a possible 22-mile day. I had to climb over three mountains – Glade Mountain at 3,900 feet, Locust Mountain and Brushy Mountain – to get to the Mt. Rogers National Recreation Area headquarters. Along the way I passed through a number of fields and had to cross over many stiles again.

In one large field where the trail traveled for more than a mile, there were about 50 cows grazing on thin grass. One big cow walked right up to me after I climbed into her field. She gave me a gentle nudge and put her wet nose under my arm. Since there had been no other hikers for months in this area, I must have been pleasant company for this big beauty as well. After talking to her for a while and petting her head, I had to move on to avoid chilling. As I continued walking the trail, which passed right through her field, she followed me. I could not believe it, but within five minutes all of her friends were along for the walk. I felt I had fifty new friends. Every time I stopped to look at them, they would all stop. At times, just for fun, I would walk ten steps and stop suddenly. They all stopped, too. We all walked together for a half hour. It was such an enjoyable time for me that I really did not want to part company. At last I came to a small footbridge that crossed a creek bordering the field. As I crossed over, I turned around to say good-bye to all my new friends, and I thought that big cow was going to cross the bridge with me. All the cows had lined up along the edge of the creek. One even walked half way into the creek. After 10 miles of hiking, I reached the closed headquarters of the recreation area, and ahead lay the highest mountain in Virginia, Mt. Rogers. I ate lunch alone on the deck outside the entrance, enjoying the sunshine that lit up the protected alcove.

Cows followed me for more than an hour through Davis Hollow near Little Bushy Mountain, VA.

I thought the cows were going to follow me over this footbridge into the next mountain range.

Wild Ponies

I continued hiking the Brushy Mountain ridge. The trail, utilizing old logging roads at times, had many ups and downs. I had not seen anyone on the trail as dusk fell slowly over the countryside, and I was still four miles from Trimpi Shelter. I donned my head lamp and walked into the ever increasing darkness. At times I lost my way in the fields. The last mile seemed like five as I finally reached the shelter trail. *"It was quiet when I arrived, and there was absolutely no wind, which seemed unusual. The clouds have moved in, and all is strangely silent. I settled into the shelter and for dinner had rice pilaf, which*

Virginia

I mixed with a small can of turkey. Now I am stuffed and have warm water in the bottles at the bottom of my sleeping bag. I have thrown sunflower seeds on the other side of the shelter so I can get a restful night's sleep and not be disturbed by mice."

I got out of the shelter early and began climbing High Point to an elevation of 4,040 feet. I noticed that I left my spoon in a shelter – again. This was the second time I did this. It started to rain steadily by early morning and continued all day long. I got chilled as my clothes and body got wetter. The trail descended past Dickey Gap and began its four-mile ascent of 4,320-foot Iron Mountain. Then it came down for two miles before climbing Pine Mountain and coming to Old Orchard Shelter. "Winds are picking up outside. I can't believe it's 45 degrees! This is the warmest night in more than a month, yet I am at the highest shelter I have stayed at in quite a while. Old Orchard Shelter is a beauty and worth a revisit! From it I can see an expansive field with great views of the mountains beyond. The temperature is rising instead of falling tonight. Wild!"

It was an amazing 50 degrees as I climbed 5,000-foot Pine Mountain the next morning. The trail went down past some horse and cattle corrals, then up Stone Mountain and down to Big Wilson Creek, which flows out of Grayson Highland State Park. The temperature rose to a sultry 60 degrees as I ascended through glorious fenced grasslands in the park where several herds of feral ponies roam free. From these grassy ridges, marked with impressive outcroppings of rock, one can see far into the countryside. It was amazing to walk through Virginia's highest mountains with all their grand scenery. Except for a few wild ponies and God, I felt as if I was alone on top of the world. After hiking along Wilbur Ridge to 5,440-foot Rhododendron Gap, I continued through open fields and rhododendron thickets. The trail then skirted the wooded summit of Mt. Rogers along Brier Ridge and descended some to Deep Gap Shelter. The deer were so numerous and were not at all skittish. "By the time I reached the side trail to Mt. Rogers, it started to get colder and windier. It began to rain about a mile from the shelter, and I arrived there just before the heavy rain fell. A cloud came by and has now settled heavily on the mountain and in the shelter."

It was foggy and windy all night long and in the morning. From the shelter I hiked down to Elk Meadow, still in clouds, then climbed Whitetop Mountain, Virginia's second highest peak. The clouds cleared for a moment as I stood near the summit, and through the mist I enjoyed grand views of the valleys below. I came down the mountain through open fields, dense forests and beautiful rhododendron thickets, crossing stiles and streams along the way. In the next five miles the trail descended about 2,300 vertical feet, then climbed again to 3,400-foot Lost Mountain. "As I sit on the Lost Mountain ridge, I can see the summit of Whitetop off in the distance. It seems so much higher than where I am now. For hundreds of miles 3,500-foot mountains have been the normal highs, but now, looking back at the majestic mountains

"I ascended through glorious fenced grasslands in the park where several herds of feral ponies roam free."

surrounding Mt. Rogers, I realize how much I have enjoyed life on peaks above 5,000 feet. As I climb the highest ridges alone with God, I feel such a sense of wonder and peace."

Railroad to Damascus

The trail off Lost Mountain descended into even larger rhododendron thickets. It then connected briefly with the Creeper Trail, which follows Whitetop Laurel Creek along an old flat railroad grade. Used originally by Native Americans, the Creeper Trail was also followed by frontiersmen including Daniel Boone and was later converted to a railroad bed. Timber harvested in the hills traveled on tracks supported by more than 100 bridges and trestles in the 93 miles between Abingdon, Virginia and the North Carolina state line. The walkway is now used for biking and hiking. The Appalachian Trail leaves the Creeper Trail and begins to climb Straight Mountain at a place where, unfortunately, I ran out of film. Near the crest of the ridge on Straight Mountain I came to Saunders Shelter, which is in a field surrounded by a thick pine grove. The shelter has a nice spring, and that night above the ridge top billions of stars twinkled in the blackness of space.

"What a day! In the early morning darkness I awoke and headed for Damascus, my next trail town. I don't know why I left so early, but I felt it was God's will. I hiked up and down Straight Mountain, up a river bank for a mile and a half and then up Iron Mountain in the dark using my head lamp. I then came down three miles into one of the best towns on the whole Appalachian Trail. It was an easy ten-mile hike, and I had tears in my eyes as I entered the quiet streets of the town in the morning light."

Damascus, Virginia is known as the friendliest town on the trail. Thousands of hikers have walked through it in the past 40 years. In May every year the town hosts the Appalachian Trail Days festival. Thousands of people converge on the community for the celebration. Many past thru-hikers, as well as those thru-hiking in the current year, attend, along with other people who love the trail. There are reunions, a talent show, outdoor equipment sales, a rodeo, dances, music and a hiker parade. Some day I will have to make the trek down there for all the festivities in this great little town. Dot's Restaurant was open, and I walked in for a meal of four eggs, four pieces of toast, two orders of hash browns and three cups of coffee – all for three dollars. I met a lot of good folk who lived in the town, then visited C.J.'s Market & Deli for groceries. At the post office I went through my package and shipped what I did not need ahead to Irwin, Tennessee, my next trail town. I also visited "The Place," a house converted into a hiker hostel and run by the United Methodist Church. It was closed for repairs. I ate a delicious fish dinner for under five dollars at Jeffreys and left town in the early afternoon as a light drizzle began to fall.

Grayson Highland State Park encompasses some of the highest terrain in Virginia.

After leaving Flint Mountain Shelter before dawn, I caught the sunrise on top of Big Butt Mountain.

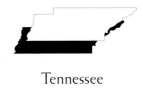
On the Mountaintop Above the Clouds

Tennessee

The walk out of Damsascus took me up 1,200 vertical feet in three miles to the Tennessee border. It was near the end of December, and I was on the 170th day of my journey. I had hiked 1,700 miles in that time. Continuing along the Holston Mountain ridge, I moved quickly in the hope of making it to Abingdon Shelter by dark and before a heavy rain came. I failed on both accounts, and the last few miles were amazingly long. After getting water from a far away spring, I settled in for the night and soon heard voices. Hikers named Scott and Dwight, on Christmas break from college, wanted to spend a night in a shelter on the Appalachian Trail. *"Today was one of my fullest. I hiked 10 miles to get into Damascus by dawn to do business. I made a few restaurant stops and then hiked another 10 miles to this shelter, where I have been talking with college students, and it is now 1:30 a.m. This means I have been awake almost 24 hours."*

Hoarfrost and clouds cover the trail in Iron Mountain Gap, TN.

Leaving late in the morning, I went along the ridge to 3,885-foot McQueens Knob. I then hiked six miles to a 4,000-foot point near Rich Knob where the trail changed direction for an ascent of the Iron Mountain ridge. I tried to enjoy my lunch at Double Springs Shelter, but all I could see was garbage. By the amount of it I judged that a large group of people had stayed there. Earlier in the day I had seen lots of trash where hunters had been waiting for deer. I carried much of it out and buried some, but in places there was so much that I just had to leave it. Throughout the day I had little energy and at times just sat down to gather strength, unable to recall any time on the trek that I was this exhausted. As daylight waned, I felt frustrated that Iron Mountain Shelter was still two miles distant. When I arrived, I was wiped out and still had to

After staying at Big Bald Mountain Shelter – which, at nearly 5,000 feet in elevation, is one of the highest shelters on the trail – I awoke before dawn and was on my way by sunrise. Within a half mile of the summit of Big Bald Mountain, I came to a clearing and realized why God had wanted me to stay at Bald Mountain Shelter that night.

"I was in so much pain

that at times I could

not walk."

walk a quarter of a mile for water. I thanked God I was there, lit my Sabbath candles and cooked a freeze-dried meal that I received from the college kids in trade for Sloppy Joe and Ramen Noodle dinners. I was looking forward to a full day's rest, for I had hiked more than 100 miles that week.

Stomach Cramps

The temperature rose for a delightful Sabbath. I wrote postcards, walked the ridge, sang praises to God and sat peacefully in the arms of a graceful tree overlooking the valley. That night, however, I awoke to a flood. Rain from a huge storm was leaking into the shelter, and when I moved to the other end, I found the roof leaking just as badly there. Looking out, I could barely see the outlines of trees. Thus, believing that a new day must be dawning, I packed up and hurriedly ate a few handfuls of Cheerios and a granola bar.

"As soon as I got my pack on, my stomach began to ache. Nevertheless, I started hiking, and eventually day came, bringing light into heavy rain, but I was in so much pain that at times I could not walk. All I could do was stop or bend over or kneel to relieve the pain. I did not know if the difficulty was from the food I ate, the water I drank or some illness. It was frustrating to be stuck in the middle of the trail, gasping in pain in the pouring rain. I traveled 16 miles in this way, sometimes feeling I would almost die. I did not eat or drink anything all day."

The trail followed the Iron Mountain ridge down to Watauga Lake. I crossed Watauga Dam in the pouring rain yet had great views of this beautiful lake and the valley. Built in 1948, the dam was the first large earth-filled hydroelectric structure in the United States. Where the trail paralleled the road into Rat Branch Recreation Area, there was quite a lot of garbage. I was of course soaked when I walked into the Rat Branch Motel and met its owner, Ed Green. Sondra and her nephew Jonathan were there to meet me. It was great to see them and to shower and put on dry clothes. When we saw that Sondra's car had died, Ed let us borrow his old red Skylark to go into town for something to eat. My stomach felt better the next morning, and I took a day off, playing Yahtzee with Jonathan and talking with Sondra and Ed. It snowed all morning, and later we went to town for more food.

The next day Jonathan and I took to the trail, beginning a three-mile ascent of Pond Mountain, the first 1.3 miles of which had an elevation gain of 1,700 feet. It was great to be with some-one on the trail again, and Jon was in good shape. Except for a few hikers near Hard Time Hollow, I had not hiked with anyone since Connecticut. Jon and I were on the ridge for a stretch, then descended steeply into Laurel Fork Gorge. For just under three miles the trail followed the Laurel Fork River in the Pine Mountain

Wilderness, where we saw many sheer cliffs and waterfalls and the ever-present rhododendron and laurel. The sides of 40-foot Laurel Falls were coated with ice, as was the rocky river shore. This would be a wonderful swimming spot for a northbounder in the spring and summer, but now it was a beautiful ice structure to be viewed only from a distance. As the trail skirted the stream along its rocky, icy shore, we had to take great care to keep from slipping and falling into the freezing water. Then we climbed out of the gorge and took a railroad bed to Dennis Cove, where Sondra was waiting. We left in darkness to get something to eat and checked into another motel.

On my own the next morning, I walked in the crisp cool air that goes with frost. The first four miles took me through woods and fields and on logging roads to the crest of White Rocks Mountain. The trail then followed a bumpy ridge with many beautiful views. From Big Pine Mountain I went down into Sugar Hollow and crossed Jones Branch Stream into Bishop Hollow — somewhat nervous as I went because hiking there was controversial. The Don Nelan Shelter in Sugar Hollow was burned down earlier that year, and at one time on parts of the trail fishing lines with hooks were tied between trees as warnings to hikers. Some local land owners were unhappy that the trail crossed their land, and this, reportedly, was how they responded. Hikers were advised not to stay overnight in the area. As I climbed the ridge before coming down into Bishop Hollow, I saw trees purposely cut down to lie across the trail, and white blazes had been either scraped off the trees or painted brown. Also, all trail signs had been removed where the trail went through fields on the descent into the hollow. Since it was approaching dark when I got to this stretch, I was frustrated and got lost many times. There were no blazes for quite a while, but I was finally able to find my way and locate some sign of the trail.

"Balds"

Sondra and Jonathan picked me up on Route 19E after this 19-mile day ended in the dark. It was raining cats and dogs the next day, so I took another break. We went into Irwin, TN for my mail drop and took a scenic drive in the country. When I set out in a few inches of snow from Bear Branch Hollow the next morning, it was drizzling. I hiked five miles through Wilder Mine Hollow and Doll Flats to the top of 5,587-foot Hump Mountain. The views from there were unbelievable. The southern Appalachians have no distinct tree line like mountains in the north, but there are many mountains with grassy tops. How they came to be this way is unknown, but they are wonderful to walk on and pro-

Sondra and Jonathan met me along Grassy Ridge and then descended to Carvers Gap.

After hiking less than three miles from Iron Mountain Gap, I could not resist the awesome peace that surrounded Cherry Gap Shelter.

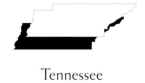

Little Hump Mountain is a "grassy bald." Although there are several theories, ecologists are not sure how mountains like this in the southern Appalachians became treeless.

"I walked up a trail covered with a half an inch of hoarfrost."

vide magnificent vistas of surrounding countryside. In deep snow the trail can easily be lost on these "balds," so a compass would be needed. From Hump Mountain the trail descends into Bradley Gap and then goes up Little Hump Mountain, where it joins and follows the state line for many miles. A southbound hiker can walk with his left leg in North Carolina and his right leg in Tennessee. The trail then enters Yellow Mountain Gap, the area where frontiersmen from Elizabethton, Tennessee defeated the British army in a pivotal Revolutionary War battle.

Farther south the trail climbs into Roan Highlands State Park and comes to 6,189-foot Grassy Ridge, the highest mountain I climbed since Mt. Washington in New Hampshire. On my way up I came upon a small, scruffy dog rolling in the grass and wondered where it came from. Once it caught sight of me, it scurried off as if I had disturbed its reign of the summit. I never saw the little fellow again. After crossing Grassy Ridge, I met Sondra and Jonathan coming from the other direction. We hiked together for two miles, going over Jane Bald at 5,807 feet and Round Bald at 5,826 feet, and descended to Carvers Gap. On high points we had walked through clouds, but at lower elevations the clouds were just above our heads, so we could see into the next mountain range and into the valleys below. From Carvers Gap we drove to Johnson City and spent the night. On the next day, a much-needed Sabbath, we ate a lot and drove to Jonesboro, the oldest town in Tennessee.

The following day Jon and I got up early and climbed to Roan High Knob. The shelter there, at 6,285 feet, is the highest on the entire Appalachian Trail. In the next two and a half miles our hike took us over Beartown Mountain and down to Hughes Gap. Then we ascended laurel-topped Little Rock Knob and went through the rhododendron and hardwood forests along Iron Mountain ridge to Clyde Smith Shelter, where we had lunch. It was a fairly warm December day, and just after we left the shelter, I noticed a hiker coming toward us wearing nylon rain pants and poncho. He introduced himself as Incense and said he began hiking from Georgia on November 18. He was the first northbounder I had seen since I met The Tortoise in Massachusetts. After talking for a while, we wished each other God's speed and continued our journeys. Jon and I climbed over many knobs in the next five miles. Then the trail descended to the road crossing at Iron Mountain Gap, where Sondra picked us up for one last night of comfortable sleeping. It was Jon's 13th birthday, and I had just entered the 13th state on my journey. So we had a celebration, cake and all. I then packed to head south in the morning, praying that God would bless Sondra and Jonathan and grant them a safe ride home.

Wintry Splendor

Leaving Iron Mountain Gap in below-freezing temperatures with clouds swirling over the ridge, I walked up a trail covered with a half an inch of hoarfrost. All the trees, branches and leaves had the same thick brilliant coating. It was a beautiful sight. On the cloudy summit of Little Bald Knob I felt weary from the weight of my 70-pound pack. For the next two miles the trail followed the ridge, then descended to Cherry Gap. Set back in a stand of hardwoods, the shelter was surrounded by fog. Clouds drifted through the forest, leaving frost in their wake. As I rested there, I felt so much at peace that I decided to stay for the rest of that day and night. After setting up camp in the shelter, I put on the new down jacket Sondra brought me from home and snuggled into my sleeping bag for a four-hour nap. When I awoke, I made a dinner of chicken noodle and potato soup, with cookies for dessert. *"Today, I believe, is January 1, and I would not want to be any place else in the world but right here on the Appalachian Trail. I awoke to a very cold morning after 15 hours of sleep. Sleeping with my hooded down jacket on inside my sleeping bag kept me warm and comfortable all night."*

Fingers of ice more than an inch high grew out of the dirt each night as the temperature on the trail dipped below freezing.

The trail to Unaka Mountain led through beautiful stands of evergreen and red spruce, and I was reminded of New England. In a few miles through the woods on the other side, the trail came to dirt roads leading to a 4,400-foot meadow called Beauty Spot. I sat in the middle of it for lunch, wishing I could stay there for days just enjoying God's glorious creation. Unfortunately, after an hour, I resigned myself to moving on. For six miles the trail came down the Unaka Mountain ridge, and I made it to Curley Maple Gap Shelter just before sundown. With the days so short, it was a blessing to arrive at a shelter, get water, visit the outhouse, get set up and begin cooking when it was still light. I awoke at dawn but did not get going for an hour. On the way to Chestoa I photographed the Jones Branch stream, the trail descending into the valley.

A new bridge over the Nolichucky River had just been completed, and I was fortunate in not having to take a four-mile relocation to the next bridge in Irwin. The trail climbed to Crest Ridge and Temple Ridge before skirting No Business Knob on a logging road. The hike had been peaceful for several days. I really sensed God's presence. Deciding to stay at No Business Knob Shelter, I sat in the sun for the rest of the day, relaxing. It rained off and on in the morning as I headed south along the east wooded slope of No Business Knob. The trail was beautiful with rhododendron as it climbed onto Flattop Mountain and came down steeply into Spivey Gap. The last half mile along Oglesby Branch was magnificent. I climbed to High Rocks and descended into Whistling Gap before the fog turned to heavy drizzle, and in another mile and a half I came to Bald Mountain Shelter. (Fairly new, this shelter is known informally as "The Carolina Condo" because it has 10 double-decker style bunks.)

Jonathan, Sondra's nephew, hiked more than 25 miles of the Appalachian Trail during his winter school vacation.

Rich Mountain can be seen in the distance from Beauty Spot on Unaka Mountain in Tennessee.

Tennessee

Hiking along High Rocks in the fog and drizzle.

Taking a break on Beauty Spot with views of the Appalachian Mountains to the south.

For some reason I felt that God's voice was quietly telling me to stay the night even though I had hiked only nine and a half miles and could easily make it to the next shelter. I felt it was a blessing to be there in heavy mist and fog. Jesus and Moses went to mountains many times to pray, and I had a precious opportunity to pray and seek God in this wilderness paradise. I seemed to have the mountain to myself, with God's presence surrounding me with loving arms, just as this thick fog enclosed the shelter. Overall I had slowed down a bit and was asking God to work His will further in my life. So I stayed, and the following morning I was magnificently blessed.

"I got to sit on top of the world today. Before sunrise, at first light, I knew it was time to get up. So I packed quickly and headed out of the shelter before the sun came over the horizon. As I began the one-mile climb to the summit of Big Bald Mountain, I knew something was different about this day and the mountain, but I couldn't tell what it was because I was walking through the forest. As soon as the trail came out of the trees and I walked onto the grassy bald, I was struck with awe. I stood silent, realizing what had happened as clouds rolled in and out all night long. In the morning light at the edge of that first meadow, a miracle unfolded before me: a sea of white as far as the eyes could see — an ocean of cloud so large that it blanketed the visible earth except for scattered islands rising out of the firmament. The world as I knew it had disappeared beneath me.

"Now I knew why God's prompting had been for me to stay on the mountain instead of going on to the next shelter in the valley. I thought of how awestruck Noah must have felt when he looked out of the window in the ark as it rested on Mt. Ararat. He saw the whole earth covered with water except for the highest mountain peaks rising up from the watery depths. All I could do was sing and praise God. Then I knelt in silence with my hands raised. The air was still. 'Glory be to God,' I said. 'Your angels rejoice before you each day because you are so great, holy, awesome and mighty. O Lord, fill me with your Spirit, mold me, guide me, and protect me so I may always see your glory.'

"For most of the day I sat and gazed at this scene, filled with wonder at God's creation and His love in allowing me to be there with Him in all that beauty. I prayed, read my Bible and looked over the world with longing in my heart. I prayed for people everywhere to live in harmony with nature and with each other. I prayed, too, that people would experience the joy I have found in walking with God through faith in Jesus. His promise of eternal life and the relationship I have with him have given me a peace that surpasses all understanding."

Although I could have stayed in that place well into the next week, I felt I had to leave, and I did so, praying that in His timing God would bring me again to a mountaintop as clear, colorful, pristine, and full of peace and glory as this one had been. The trail down followed a beautiful ridge, crossed scenic farmlands into Sam's Gap, then climbed High Rock Mountain and over Lick Rock. I moved through forests and fields and on logging roads to the place where Laurel Branch flows by Boone Cove Road. Within a few more miles the trail came to Flint Mountain Shelter, where I

spent two nights including a Sabbath pondering recent events. From the shelter with one candle burning, I looked out into the darkness and thought how strange it was to be alone. There I was, miles from people. I had spent nearly a hundred nights alone. Days went by and I would see no one. I guess I didn't mind it anymore. God always had something to teach me, but right then I was thinking it would be nice to be with someone.

"What a great day off! I relaxed in the shelter most of the morning, then took walks around the area. Suddenly, six hikers from the Knoxville area came up the trail. Ronnie, Nick, Dennis, Bill, Rick and Buddy were out for a week, hiking south to Hot Springs, North Carolina. We all had a great time that night chatting around a campfire, and we went to sleep late. For some reason I awoke very early and noticed a bright half moon in the sky. After praying I decided to pack up and head out. Ronnie got up and started a fire, and we talked for a while in the predawn darkness. He offered his help at any time. I said good-bye to all the guys and prayed that God would give them a safe, enjoyable journey."

Sunrise, Sunset

I sang by the light of the moon as I hiked the trail to Big Butt Mountain. By the time I reached the summit, the sun was casting an orange glow on the horizon. The sunrise was glorious – first pink, then deep orange, then flaming yellow – and it was wonderful to hear the birds' first calls to one another. When I arrived at Big Rocks, though, clouds had covered the earth again, and I could see nothing in the valley but a sea of white. After a few more miles through fields and woods, I came to Jerry Cabin Shelter, which had a phone and light switch – put there, I believe, to amuse hikers. I went on for five miles at over 4,000 feet on the ridges of Bald Mountain, traveling in the beautiful Pisgah National Forest, then descended to Little Laurel Shelter, which has an excellent piped spring, and had lunch. The temperature had risen into the 50s, and it was wonderful to be on the trail.

From the shelter the trail continued to follow the Tennessee-North Carolina border, coming down steeply to Allen Gap on Route 70. I drank a Mountain Dew at a gas station before heading up Spring Mountain. I climbed over three good-sized knobs and in four miles reached Spring Mountain Shelter, a beautiful facility in a wooded notch at 3,300 feet. I had hiked more than 21 miles to reach it and planned to stay the night. In visiting the unusual open-aired privy with no walls, I sat looking out over the pristine countryside from the side of Spring Mountain. I don't know exactly what happened then, but suddenly I had a surge of energy and I felt like going all the way to Hot Springs. This was ludicrous, especially since my hiking day had begun before sunrise. I prayed and then wrote in the register, filled with excitement and not knowing what lay ahead that night.

It was already late afternoon, and I had 10 miles to hike, including a major mountain and two minor ones. I hurried as darkness fell, reached the summit of Rich Mountain (3,643 feet), then

I was hoping for someone to talk to on a Sabbath at Flint Mountain Shelter, and in came six great guys from Tennessee.

As I neared the Big Bald summit, the mountains were covered with a thick blanket of clouds as far as eyes could see. Only the highest peaks in the southern Appalachians were visible – rising like islands in the sea of white. I was alone with God in a magnificent scene on top of the world.

On the summit a great sense of peace descended upon Big Bald Mountain. I could see the sun slowly rise just above the horizon.

"I am now sitting comfortably on a thick bed of pine needles in the middle of the Appalachian Trail".

went by head lamp for hours. My feet hurt three miles before I reached Tanyard Gap, but I continued, the trail following Mill Ridge to Lovers Leap Ridge and then dropping steeply to the French Broad River. From the Lovers Leap Overlook I saw the twinkling lights of Hot Springs. I crossed the river and reached the town just after 9 p.m. Everything was closed, so I got to the Inn at Hot Springs as quickly as I could. It, too, looked closed when I saw it, and I knew the Jesuit-run hiker's hostel was closed for the winter. I walked up to the white Victorian house owned by Elmer Hall and knocked on the door. To my surprise, Elmer came out from the kitchen. He really looked me over. Having seen no thru-hikers for months, he found it hard to believe I was a southbounder from Maine and had hiked all day and night to reach Hot Springs. Yet he graciously invited me in. I took a long hot shower while Elmer set out a vegetarian soup, which I enjoyed with bagels and tea. *"I am still not sure why God has me here, but I am thankful for this wonderful inn, cozy room and comfortable bed."*

Patterns of hardwoods along No Business Knob.

In prayer in front of Lemon Gap Shelter.

Cammerer Ridge in Great Smoky Mountains National Park near Davenport Gap on the North Carolina-Tennessee border. A huge storm came in from the south like a tidal wave, filling the valley with clouds and bringing a hard rain that lasted through the night.

Walking Through a Crystal Ice Palace

North Carolina

What a day! In the morning I awoke to a rooster call and walked to the Trail Cafe for breakfast. I also visited the bank, sorted through my mail and food boxes, and sent unneeded items back home. Then I went to the Trail Cafe for lunch and visited a hardware store, talking with the owner, Mr. Gentry, for an hour. Once I did laundry, got groceries and made needed phone calls, it was dark, so I brought my clothes and food back to the Inn at Hot Springs and tried to go out for a bite to eat – but there was no restaurant open after 7 p.m. I came back to the inn, made a peanut butter and jelly sandwich for dinner and packed my pack. In the morning I walked to the cafe for one last breakfast. Then I returned to the inn to say good-bye and thanks to Elmer, Freddy and Gretchen, who were ordering herbs for the upcoming hiking and tourist season.

The trail headed uptown, passing the Jesuit hostel and ascending into the woods to the ridge on Deer Park Mountain. It went up, up and up for almost 10 miles until, finally, it reached the summit of Bluff Mountain at 4,686 feet. From there it went down to Kale Gap and up to Walnut Mountain and one of the oldest shelters on the Appalachian Trail. It was just dusk when I arrived there, and a stiff wind was blowing in 40-degree air. Though I was cold, I was enjoying the night hikes, so I donned my head lamp two and a half miles farther, coming down to Lemon Gap and a new shelter called Roaring Brook. I was glad to come off the windy heights and get situated by a stream that flowed through dense rhododendron and other foliage. I asked God to continue to guide me and move in a special way in my life.

Early in the morning I was awakened by mice working on a popcorn ball I received in the mail. Unable to get my teeth into it, I had left it on the shelter floor to keep the mice busy, and during

Hoarfrost near Davenport Gap.

An approaching storm brought heavy rain which leaked into Cosby Knob Shelter all night

the night they got through half of it. I walked six miles in clouds along the Max Patch Mountain ridge, crossing streams and moving through rhododendron and hemlock onto the open meadow of Buckeye Ridge. I was still in blowing clouds as I neared the summit of Max Patch, but suddenly the fog cleared and the sun began to burn off the haze. The whole earth was open before me in another display of God's magnificent glory. I relaxed for the rest of the afternoon.

"How can I praise God enough? Here I sit, on top of Max Patch, a beautiful bald mountain, with a blanket of white clouds covering the valleys as far as the eye can see. The highest peaks, showing through the clouds, look like long pyramids in a sea of white. Sixty miles to the south lies Great Smoky Mountains National Park and to the east Mt. Mitchell, the highest mountain in the eastern Appalachians. Mountaintops are jutting up through the mist like giant sentinels. Again, I am on top of the world with God! It is awesome."

Sweet Fellowship

While eating lunch on Max Patch, I saw another small dog. It sniffed around for a while, then took off downhill. In time I left the summit and descended along the ridge into the clouds. Within a few hours I could not believe how cold it was – in the lower 30s with dense fog, rain and a 20 m.p.h. wind. On top it had been in the 50s with just a breeze. The trail went down six miles to Deep Gap, which was enveloped in fog and darkness. Groundhog Creek Shelter is on the edge of an open field with a creek meandering through nearby woods. I felt nervous coming to the shelter with only the light of my head lamp shining in the mist. It was a little spooky. I was grateful to see that the structure was empty. It took me two tries to find the stream in the darkness. Dinner was Lipton Soup with turkey and potatoes. Before I went to sleep, I thanked God for another glorious mountaintop experience.

I woke early, still in fog, and climbed Snowboard Mountain, the summit of which has an FAA transmission station. I could have spent more time there, but the wind was stiff and I had to go six miles to reach the Pigeon River and Great Smoky Mountains National Park. I had contacted Jeff and Suzie from Knoxville, the couple I had met near Griffith Lake in Vermont. Jeff was going to pick me up in the afternoon at the Big Creek Ranger Station in Davenport Gap. I got lost following an old trail near the bottom of the mountain and needed to backtrack. After crossing the river, the trail rises for about a mile and a half to Tobes Creek and State Line Branch, coming out to Davenport Gap at 1,975 feet. I walked a mile down a dirt road to the ranger station and while waiting for Jeff I fed a horse and wrote postcards.

It was great to see Jeff again. We talked non-stop about what the Lord had been doing in our lives, and within minutes, it seemed, we arrived at his house in Knoxville. Suzie had prepared a super dinner. I stuffed myself as politely as I could. We had a wonderful conversation until I could hardly keep my eyes open. It was after midnight when I retired to a comfortable bed. For the next

"Mountaintops are jutting up through the mist like giant sentinels. Again, I am on top of the world with God! It is awesome."

few days Jeff had my time booked: speaking engagements at Christian gatherings, church meetings, friends over for dinner, a men's retreat near Gatlinburg as well as a University of Tennessee versus Kentucky basketball game. I had never seen such enthusiasm in one place as was shown in that gymnasium. Football and basketball are big – very big – in this part of the country. The contrast between that crowd of more than 50,000 cheering people and life on the trail was amazing. I was overwhelmed by the noise.

In those days I often went to bed exhausted, but I was thankful for the chance to meet wonderful people who made my visit in Knoxville a blessing.

We left the house early Sunday morning to attend a church at which Jeff and Suzie's son-in-law was an associate pastor. After that service we went to their church, where I spoke to the choir about my life and journey. The worship service was wonderful. Afterward we had a great lunch and relaxed until the evening service. Then we ate again, and I put my worldly possessions back into my pack. I enjoyed this comfortable living and did not have to be concerned about the cold whistling outside at the beginning of January.

The Great Smokies

Early in the morning we all prayed before I was driven back to Davenport Gap. I asked for God's greatest blessing on Jeff and Suzie's family. I stood by the trail sign for a few moments getting my bearings and trying to get up the energy for a 3,000-foot vertical climb in just four miles to reach the ridge of the Smoky Mountains. Just over 70 miles of the Appalachian Trail are within the boundary of the great park I was approaching. I began the slow ascent in a cold sweat, and when I reached the crest of Cammerer Ridge, the mercury had dropped into the low 20s, layering many trees along the way with hoarfrost. The trail followed the high ridge to 5,050-foot Sunup Knob, dipped into Low Gap and climbed again for a mile before coming to Cosby Knob Shelter. Walking in snow, my feet got very cold in the last few miles. I could not wait to get into my sleeping bag.

The Smoky Mountains are beautiful. Many of its forests and ridges reminded me of those in Maine. As I left the shelter in the morning, heading for the north slope of Mt. Guyot (the highest point of my hike so far at 6,360 feet), the wind picked up. A storm front was rolling in from the southeast, its cloud line resembling a tidal wave trying to get over the mountains. In time the wind began to howl and gust to 50 m.p.h. or more. All I could do was stand and lean into it. Trees were being whipped back and forth. The ground seemed to be shaking. As I got above 6,000 feet again, I walked into clouds, and rain fell intermittently on the beautiful balsam and spruce forest through which I was moving.

The trail descended to Big Cove Gap. I ate lunch at Tri-Corner Knob Shelter. In the growing storm I still had a five-mile trek over Mt. Chapman and Mt. Sequoyah to reach Peck's Corner Shelter. I arrived just before dark and was arranging my things on

North Carolina

Resting on Max Patch with only the highest of surrounding peaks visible.

Clouds completely cover the earth again as far as the eye can see on Max Patch.

The Appalachian Trail crosses Max Patch with views of the Great Smoky Mountains National Park to the south.

the lower deck when the storm broke savagely overhead. Surprisingly at this high elevation, it only rained – even though the temperature was in the low 30s. Within an hour after I fell asleep, water was plopping on my sleeping bag, and I had to move five times to find the shelter's only dry corner. By morning the rain had stopped, but the shelter was filled with water and mouse droppings. Shelters in the Smokies are different from those elsewhere on the trail. For protection against bears, hikers are locked behind fence doorways. At this time of year, of course, the bears were presumably hibernating, but also, there are no outhouses at these shelters. Bathroom needs must be taken care of in the woods, at least 100 feet away from water sources.

I thought the storm would clear, but it rained off and on most of the day. I felt achy as I traveled through virgin stands of balsam and spruce on the way to Icewater Spring Shelter, passing by a magnificent rock outcropping called Charlie's Bunion. It was on a precipitous side trail, and with the wind and rain I was prohibited from adventuring onto cliffs. Tired, I stayed at Icewater Spring, whose stone shelter, at 5,890 feet in elevation, is one of the highest on the Appalachian Trail. The first hikers I had met in a long time came in at the end of the day. It was below freezing all night, and wind-driven clouds rolled in. It began to snow.

When I awoke in the morning, the wind had died down, and nature had left a glorious imprint: crystal-white hoarfrost shimmering on all the trees. Everywhere I looked was a picture-perfect postcard. I could have taken photographs all day over the next extraordinary miles of trail, which were like a crystal ice palace in a winter wonderland. God's glorious presence covered this frost-covered ridge with such beauty, grace and peace. I can only imagine how beautiful heaven will be. The trail descended for miles to Newfound Gap, where a road cuts through the center of the park.

There were many cars and people milling about, and I was continually asked about my journey and heavy pack. I could not wait to get back to the peace and quietness of the wilderness.

From Newfound Gap I had a seven-plus-mile hike over Mt. Collins and Mt. Love. Finally I was climbing the highest mountain on the trail, 6,643-foot Clingman's Dome. It, too, was covered with a heavy layer of hoarfrost and was encircled by stands of balsam, Frazer firs and rare mountain cranberry. The only way to view the whole park from this summit was to climb the cement observation deck. The temperature dropped all day, going to the low teens with the wind gusting to more than 30 m.p.h. on the summit. I was the only person there, and the wind blew through to my skin as I looked out over the southern Appalachians. I tried to take pictures, but my fingers became numb, so I had to get off the tower quickly. It was late in the afternoon, and I knew I would get to Double Spring Gap Shelter after dark. As I came down to the lower summit of Mt. Buckley (6,582 feet), the trail followed a narrow ridge. Double Spring Gap Shelter is in a beautiful field with a spring nearby. While I was cooking dinner, mice came out in droves, and I literally had to kick one out of my pack. *"It is 20 degrees now as I sit out-*

The Appalachian Trail begins to freeze near Mt. Guyot in the Great Smoky Mountains National Park.

The trail turned to ice along Mt. Kephart
after the storm left.

It was a cold night at Ice Water Spring Shelter.

Hoarfrost more than an inch thick covered trees and the trail all the way into Newfound Gap. I walked through a
crystal ice palace for miles, just praising God.

The summit of Clingman's Dome in Great Smoky Mountains National Park is covered by hoarfrost. The 6,643-foot mountain is the highest point on the Appalachian Trail. I came to it on a beautiful day – although a 35 m.p.h. wind was blowing and the temperature was about 15 degrees.

North Carolina

Clouds fill the lower valleys along the trail on Cammerer Ridge.

side the shelter. The stars are the best I have seen anywhere in the world. With only a sliver of a moon on a crystal clear night, there seem to be a million stars. I passed another milestone today by hiking over the trail's highest peak. Praise God for His faithfulness."

The trail crossed 5,607-foot Siler's Bald with its stunning views of the southern Smokies. Then deciduous hardwoods began to replace coniferous forests, with magnificent stands of beech trees lining the trail for the next four miles. I ate lunch in Derrick Knob Shelter knowing there were six miles and three mountains between me and Spence Field Shelter. Due to its large elevation gains and losses, this section of trail was more strenuous than any I had experienced in a long time. I finally made the 5,527-foot summit of Thunderhead, but as I took my pack off to use as a tripod for my camera, I heard a cracking sound. The pack frame folded over limply in the shape of a wide V. I could not believe it. Broken again! I was at a loss as to what to do. All I knew is that God has a reason for everything.

Fortunately, I was only a mile from the shelter, and I made it just at sundown. When I arrived at the shelter, to my surprise, it was filled with hikers, more than I had seen since Vermont, and there was a fire in the fireplace. Rich, whose trail name was Equipto Man, helped me fix the frame so I could hike, and he gave me some of his trail food. That night we had some unusual guests: skunks. Actually these adorable looking animals live in several shelters in the Smokies, coming and going as they please. There seemed to be two skunks living in this shelter, and they were looking for handouts. When a hiker left his pack on the ground, I saw a skunk crawl into it and disappear. We talked until midnight, and then I had a fitful sleep because I drank too much coffee.

I hoped to rest the next day, but by mid-afternoon 12 hikers sauntered in, then another four, followed by 15 kids. Rich and I felt we should not take up spaces, so we packed up and walked to Russell Field Shelter, two and a half miles away. The hike was mostly downhill, so it was relaxing. It rained the last mile, and when we arrived, we were greeted by two parole officers, Don and Pat, out hiking for the weekend. All evening we ate and ate, and I was stuffed by the time I finished my spaghetti dinner. This shelter also was inhabited by skunks. Most did not smell skunky, but at times they gave one another a little spray when playing. If they came in from outside, they might have had to spray a predator, which would bring in a lingering smell. As I was sleeping on my back in the middle of the night, a skunk crawled over my face, and unfortunately it was stinky one. I awoke with a fright and was stunned as the animal sat on my face. I shot up. The skunk flew into the air, landing near my feet with its tail up, pointed at me. It looked back at me for a few seconds and, by God's grace, walked off the lower bunk without retaliation. I had many mice crawl on me during this journey, and they were not too bad, but this was unbelievable!

A skunk that lived in the shelter crawled onto my face in the middle of the night.

This evergreen stands guard near the cement tower on top of Clingman's Dome.

While many springs and streams near Tyre Top Ridge in North Carolina were frozen, water moved melodically beneath the ice. God's fingerprints and the infinite variety in nature can be seen in the beauty of scenes such as these.

Hiking in snow near Cold Spring Shelter.

Snow on the trail became deeper as I climbed higher into the Stecoah Range.

"At peace and filled with worshipful awe at God's presence, I am being lulled to sleep by the sound of the water."

I awoke at dawn after another fitful sleep. I prayed and ate a large breakfast before heading across the ridge that would end my wonderful journey in the Smokies. Coming down into Ekaneetlee Gap, I scared a number of wild boars, strange looking animals that had dug up the whole area on top of the ridge to get at the roots of small trees and plants. I wondered if trees would ever grow there again. I then ascended 4,520-foot Doe Knob, where the trail abruptly changed direction (leaving the Smokies main ridge) and headed south on a spur. It began to rain as I came to the top of Shuckstack Mountain. I descended steeply to the Little Tennessee River, crossing the 480-foot high Fontana Dam, which was built by the Tennessee Valley Authority for hydroelectric power during World War II. Circling the closed visitor center in 40-degree rain, I met hikers from Georgia who warned me of a coming cold front. Fortunately, rest rooms near the top of the dam were opened and heated. I sat on the floor to warm up, snacking and pondering my broken pack frame. It would take a few days for a new frame to arrive, and I did not want to wait at the shelter near the dam for two or three days in below freezing weather. Then I remembered Ronnie, one of the hikers I met north of Hot Springs two weeks earlier. He said he would be happy to help me, and when I called, he gladly agreed to come. Praise God!

As I walked toward Fontana Lake Shelter, I met a park ranger named Ray. We talked about the Lord and prayed together, and this lifted my spirit. The shelter, which sleeps 20 and has picnic tables, a water spigot and a heated rest room, is known as the Fontana Hilton. There I met Kodi, a young man who had hiked the trail in 1986 and now, with only 50 dollars to his name, was looking for work. He drove me to Route 28, where I would meet Ronnie.

Kodi and I talked for a few hours in his car while waiting for Ronnie to arrive. I prayed that God would support Kodi and help him find a job. While we were talking, a police officer came by thinking we were causing trouble. We talked with him for a while before Ronnie and his friend Rick showed up in a green Volkswagen van, and we began the two-hour drive to Ronnie's house in Sevierville. It was wonderful to see these guys again. We had a great time talking about our hikes to Hot Springs. They could not believe I hiked in one day a distance they did in five. When we arrived at Ronnie's house, we talked more, and I slept on the den floor, thanking God for the warmth and kindness I was enjoying.

Snow was falling by mid-morning. I called Kelty, and a service rep said a new frame as well as some replacement straps would soon be on the way. The next day Ronnie and I went to Hartford, Tennessee to visit Fred, a fifth-generation Appalachian farmer who sold crafts on the side. After our visit, we took Ronnie's handiwork, 25 wooden toy trucks, to another place to sell. We made it to the Sevierville post office just before it closed, finding that my pack frame had arrived! Back home, Ronnie made a beef chuck and gravy meal, and I fixed my pack and reloaded it. That night Ronnie gave me venison jerky and homemade jelly for the trail, and he and

his wife, Julie, talked with me late into the night. Morning came quickly.

Ronnie and I arrived at Fontana Village before noon. I had four boxes awaiting me – from Steve and Lisa in Pennsylvania, Melissa and Valerie (former students of mine) in Massachusetts, Jeff and Suzie in Tennessee, and, of course, my next mail drop. There was also a package of letters, inspiring notes and drawings from the children at the Solomon Schechter Day School, where I taught sixth grade and physical education before beginning my hike. The children, tracking my journey, were moving a little moleskin "hiking man" southward on a map. I sent them letters from each town I visited, and it was great to read their letters to me. It took over an hour to work through all this. (I could not find the travelers checks I expected to receive in the mail drop, and I had only two dollars!) I gave extra food to Ronnie, said a thankful good-bye and prayed for God's blessing on him and his family.

Cold

I sang praises to God as I left Fontana Dam. Most of the trail to Yellow Creek Mountain was blanketed with snow, and I made it to Cable Gap Shelter before the sun set. Once again my pack weighed close to 80 pounds, but the new straps felt great. I was feeling both excited and sad in contemplating the end of my wilderness experience. An air of great anticipation welled up in me as I moved farther south. It was hard to believe I was using my last trail guide and coming to the final segment of the journey. *"Jeff (The Lummox) sent me a small hymn book, and I have enjoyed singing tonight in the warmth and comfort of my sleeping bag. My melodies ramble across the bleak snow-covered forest to the waiting ears of any nocturnal creatures that might be listening. When I pause in singing, all I can hear is a babbling brook near the shelter and the incredible silence of nature. At peace and filled with worshipful awe at God's presence, I am being lulled to sleep by the sound of the water."*

It was 18-degrees and cloudy as I began my trek through the famous Stecoah Mountains. Once known for its difficulty, this section of trail had been relocated to ease some of the ascents and descents, but there were still many ups and downs. It was a blessing to be hiking in the snow, though. The mountains and trees were gorgeous, and there was not much wind, but it was very cold – and what a difficult trail! It was a trial of patience, strength and sheer existence.

"This was probably the most difficult day for me in over a thousand miles of hiking. All 15 miles were either up or down. The last six miles from Stecoah Gap were extremely hard. I thought I would not make it up Cheoah Bald at 5,062 feet. The trail went up forever, especially as night began to fall. What a struggle! Of course, the 80 pounds on my back had something to do with the challenge. Also, the half foot of snow on the trail made the footing slippery. My feet were numb, and I felt I was going in slow motion up every mountain and hill. I finally reached Sassafras Gap Shelter a few hours after sundown. The wind, blowing in from the north on this half-moon star-filled night, had begun to pick up, and I could hear it howling on the ridge above me. Fortunately, the shelter is in a hollow on the mountain's south side. I almost did not have the energy to get

"Cold? What is cold? with frozen boots and frozen water bottles, I did not want to take one step out of my cocoon."

water from the icy spring. It was 20 degrees when I arrived, and now, after dinner, it has dropped to 11. I forgot to put my boots inside my sleeping bag. They are frozen solid. It was a difficult chore to squeeze my feet into them, walk to the privy and sit on a frozen seat with a 25 m.p.h. wind blowing around the hollow. I just heard an owl give a loud, long Hooooooh in this frozen wilderness."

Cold? What is cold? With frozen boots and frozen water bottles, I did not want to take one step out of my cocoon. My fingertips and toes came close to frostbite that night. There was a painful thawing out period for each digit for an hour after I got in my sleeping bag. It stayed cold, and the snow covered my boots and remained there for most of the day. A Sabbath was coming up, and in view of the frigid weather I decided to try to stay at the Nantahala Outdoor Center instead of in a shelter – but I did not know if the center would take a charge card. I would not be getting more cash until my next trail town. The day's hike was truly on my side: only one uphill climb to Swim Bald at 4,720 feet, followed by a steep descent to the Nantahala River at 1,723 feet.

I photographed frozen waterfalls until my fingers nearly froze off. As I came quickly off the ridge, I met an old time hunter named Marvin who loved hiking in the woods. We talked for a while and shared venison jerky. A beautiful gold and white dog bounded up the trail and hung around while we chatted. When we parted company, the dog followed Marvin. He told me to call her, and for the next few miles into Wesser she followed me. As I got close to the river, I assumed I would see signs of the dog's owner, but I did not. Crossing the bridge, I watched people in kayaks run a slalom course. Anyone I asked about the dog had never seen her, so I kept her with me, and she tagged along as if she were mine. I was thankful to learn that the hostel had a vacancy and would accept a Mastercard. I took the dog to my room, having been told that I would be contacted if its owner made inquiry. I then took a wonderful warm shower.

Later a worker at the hostel came in to say a woman had called about the dog, overjoyed to know someone found her. I was happy that the owner and dog would be reunited. A half hour later Dick and Linda came by to pick up "Brenda," and we talked about their farm. In the afternoon I did laundry, cooked and ate dinner and fell asleep. In the morning I walked to a riverside restaurant and had the best veggie-cheese omelet (with home fries) that I had tasted in years. Then I took a long walk, read the Bible and prayed and talked to people. It was a relaxing day. I went to bed early to be ready for the next day's ascent.

Before leaving the next morning, I returned to the restaurant for breakfast. In a steep four-mile climb I reached a rocky outcrop called The Jump Up. In another two and a half miles I came to the 4,627-foot summit of Wesser Bald and had great views of the surrounding area from a rebuilt fire tower. Snow on the trail deepened as I came up and diminished as I went down into Tellico Gap. At 4,920 feet on the south side of Copper Ridge Bald, Cold Spring Shelter was covered by four inches of snow. Just after I arrived, more snow began to come down. With fluffy flakes fluttering out of the sky all night, the forest was tranquil. *"It has been a privilege to be here walking with God. His peace truly reigns supreme in the wilderness and in my heart."*

Reaching Out

North Carolina

*I*n the morning I set out for Wayah Bald and seven miles later was climbing its huge stone tower. It was a cold sunny day, and views of the snow-covered Smokies to the north were magnificent. On a two-mile hike along the ridge to Wine Spring Bald, I met a singing hiker named Bill. We talked for a while, and then he invited me for coffee. "How can we have coffee on the trail here at 5,000 feet with snow all around us?" I asked. "There certainly isn't a McDonald's around." Bill said there was a spring farther south on the trail where we could make a fire. Since that was the direction I was hiking, I agreed. In about a quarter of a mile we came to Wine Spring, where we collected wood, built a fire and heated water. For the entire afternoon we sat at the fire talking about life and God. Bill decided to spend the night there. I felt I should stay with him, but my day's schedule called for me to reach Siler Bald Shelter, four miles down the trail. I set out, leaving Bill by the fire, but half way down Wine Spring Bald I stopped in my tracks, a strong voice within saying "Stop!" I even felt it in my heart. Immediately I said out loud, "You're right, Lord. I need to stay with Bill." I turned around, hiked back up the mountain and told Bill that I was going to spend the night with him. Then I set my tent up, and we gathered more wood before cooking a big pot of potato stew.

This old hunter and I shared venison near the Nantahala River in Wesser, NC.

Bill had been homeless for many years. He had biked across the country, visiting Indian reservations, and then lived in a van for years. Recently, while living with his mother in Georgia, he had decided to try the trail. All he carried was a bed roll and an old canvas pack, half-filled, and there I was with my fancy gear and bulging pack. The dichotomy was startling. We talked late under the stars. When I wrote down his mother's address and phone number, he said I was the first person to show an interest in him in a long time. Inwardly I prayed that God would protect and bless him, and since the temperature was dipping into the teens, I hoped he would be warm enough in his bed roll. I was also able to share my faith in Jesus with Bill and to pray for him and his family. So I knew this was where God wanted me that night.

Bill said there was a campsite at Wine Spring just down the trail. We made a big fire and enjoyed each other's company.

In the morning Bill made another huge fire. We talked as I packed, and after breakfast and another prayer I left for Wayah Gap. For some reason I felt exhausted. I had no energy. How was I going to climb 5,216-foot Siler Bald? I decided to sit and have an early lunch. Maybe that would raise my energy level. As I began to climb, the temperature rose to almost 50 degrees. I praised the Lord as I sat atop the grassy bald looking in all directions. In the next 13 miles on the way to Wallace Gap and Albert Mountain, the trail went up and down many times. When I arrived at Rock Gap Shelter, just south of the gap, I was tired and wanted to stay, but the shelter was uncomfortably close to a road so I went on to Big Spring Shelter, five miles up the trail. *"It was a great hike. The mountain laurel and rhododendron thickets were magnificent. Miles of rhododendron tunnels lined the trail, and beautiful streams crossed it and followed alongside. As I climbed to higher elevations along the ridge, fog swept in, and dimming light ended another precious day. Right now I am enjoying a cup of*

I camped with Bill on Wine Spring Bald on a below freezing night.

211

potato soup and watching the rain outside. *God is faithful and all sufficient. I feel His presence so close and sense His purpose in my life."*

"The temperature dropped from 45 degrees to 21, and my boots froze solid."

Fatigue

I woke up exhausted and extremely hungry and did not understand why. The previous day was a hard push, but I did have a filling meal. Outside it was pouring rain, and it seemed to be taking me hours to get moving. I would have to climb Albert Mountain again when it was not raining. I tried but could not make it to Standing Indian Shelter, more than 14 miles down the trail. When I came to Carter Gap Shelter, I knew I needed to stay because I was fatigued and shaking and realized these were the first signs of hypothermia. I had only hiked seven miles. The shelter roof had one large leak and many small ones, so I set up my tent inside it and lay in my sleeping bag looking out at the cold rain. The previous few days had been physically demanding. I never felt so tired and wondered if my body was getting burned out from the seven months of hiking. I had lost a lot of weight and felt as if I was beginning to use my body for energy.

My sleeping bag was damp again, losing loft. I was feeling cooler at night. Also, my food was running out, and I had 60 miles to hike to get to Neels Gap and my final mail drop. I could not make that with the food I had.

So I sought God and thanked Him for the shelter, even with all its leaks. Just before dark hikers named Joe, Lonnie and Jim joined me in the shelter. What a surprise! They worked as nurses in Georgia and were out for three days during time off. It was great having company, but unfortunately for them, they had the leaky side of the shelter.

Overnight the temperature dropped from 45 degrees to 21, and my boots froze solid. Before leaving the shelter in the morning, the three guys asked me if I wanted some food. They were leaving the trail that day and did not need it. I thanked them sincerely, realizing that if I had moved farther along the trail the day before, I would have missed this offer. After five miles of uphill hiking, I reached the top of 5,498-foot Standing Indian Mountain, then climbed down to the shelter for lunch. It was cold and windy. In the shelter I found three potatoes and four onions that the nurses must have left the day before. Praise God! Then I hiked five miles across Blue Ridge and came down to the A-framed Muskrat Shelter.

"I still have that burnt-out feeling. Some moments on the trail today I loved. At other times I was just exhausted. I wonder if I am becoming vitamin deficient. When I arrived here, I saw five eggs in the fire pit. Those guys must have left these as well. I couldn't believe it! Only one egg had been pecked open, and the others looked great, so I quickly boiled water and cooked them as fast as my stove would heat them. I ate three of the eggs as fast as I could, feeling I had never tasted anything so good. I also found a can of corn in the shelter, which I added to the potatoes and onions along with a package of Millie's Peas and Pasta soup. My two-quart pot was filled to the brim. I feasted from it for an hour and was the fullest I had been in a long time — but I would not have passed up dessert if I had had some."

As I came down Swim Bald Ridge, I could see the Nantahala River in the valley. I knew I had to cross the river and then climb back up into the Nantahala Mountain Range.

The trail was shrouded in fog as I hiked out of Neels Gap.

Journey's End to a New Beginning

Georgia

After settling into the cold shelter for the night, I read the Bible and wrote in my journal. *"For some reason I am constantly hungry. With the intense cold and heavy hiking, my body must not be getting enough food. Maybe I have a tapeworm. Oh well, I praise God for His presence and the strength He gives me each day. He is miraculously supplying enough food to sustain me and has met all my needs. I am just trusting in Him. Tomorrow, if He is willing, I will be in Georgia, which is hard to believe. I have only 80 or so miles to go."*

On a 15-degree morning at Muskrat Shelter, I did not want to get out of my sleeping bag, but with the little food I had left in my pack, I had to keep going. The next day would be a Sabbath, which I hoped would rejuvenate me. I ate enough for breakfast, but after hiking for a little while I was exhausted again. When I finally arrived at Bly Gap, I came to the large old gnarly oak that stands in the grassy field there. It was leafless. I cried a little and praised God for His faithfulness in enabling me to make it that far.

This place, near the border of North Carolina and Georgia, is significant to any thru-hiker. Northbounders are leaving their first state when they pass through; southbounders are entering their last state. It was a beautiful cloudless 40-degree day. From where I sat beneath the branches of the tree, snacking in the morning sunshine, the sky was a deep, velvety blue. It was February 1, and I had hiked 2,070 miles of the Appalachian Trail.

To the south the trail entered the Chattahoochee National Forest, still following the Blue Ridge and coming to many mountains, knobs and gaps on the way to its southern terminus, Springer Mountain. The next three miles descended easily to Blue Ridge

A tranquil peace filled the air as I hiked near the cloud-covered summit of Blood Mountain. Springer Mountain was just 30 miles to the south.

Sunset on the Appalachian Trail as I descend Courthouse Bald Mountain. As I hiked into my last state, with Springer Mountain coming closer, I was filled with many different emotions.

This tree in Bly Gap is often photographed because it signifies the Georgia-North Carolina border. People hiking north are leaving their first state, and southbounders have only 88 miles remaining on their journey to Springer Mountain, Georgia.

"I could not believe the awesome, colorful display of the grand sunset that evening."

Gap, then I climbed As Knob and followed the ridge to Plumorchard Gap Shelter. I thought of staying there, but that would have made only a seven-and-a-half-mile day. There was a lot of the daylight left, so I decided to go on to Addis Creek Shelter, 11 miles farther. The last four of these miles was an uphill climb to Powell Mountain and 4,276-foot Kelly Knob. I came to the shelter as the last rays of the sun filled the mountainside with its warm, yellow glow. Thanking God for the strength to get there, I set up camp for my two-night stay. This was a thousand feet lower in elevation than I had been for many days, and I hoped the severely cold weather would be gone for a while.

"On this Sabbath I have thought a lot about the wonders of water. I am sitting beside South Fork Stream, listening to its babbling voices and watching it flow by — continually, consistently, always in balance, yet always changing. It is amazing how deep mountain wells continue to pour sweet, life-giving water into springs, creeks, brooks and rivers. There must be vast reservoirs beneath the earth's surface that we will never know about. In the story of Noah and the ark, wells opened up and water poured out onto the earth, along with the 40 days of rain, to cover the whole earth. I know I need water to live every day.

"In the Bible, people who delight in God are described as trees planted by water so they can always bear fruit, even when drought or difficult times come upon them. They have strength and nourishment and can stand strong in trials. God's presence flows through everything, as life-giving water moves over the earth. I pray that I will be able to tap into this flow daily, that it will fill me and pour from me in a way that will be spiritually uplifting to people God places in my life. I don't know why, but a sacred peace beyond all understanding has descended upon this place and has remained all day. I believe that God chose this beautiful spot in this secluded ravine with a rushing stream surrounded by majestic mountains for me to seek Him on this special day."

As the light of day began to dim, a holy quietness descended upon the ravine, and I returned to the shelter.

Heel and Toe Problems

In the evening of the Sabbath, I sat in front of the shelter eating soup. It was great to watch the day end with darkness filling every corner of the forest surrounding me. Later that night, however, I could not believe what the mice did. I had put some raisin fudge and leftover spaghetti in the corner of the shelter for the mice to eat. In the middle of the night, needing to visit the outdoor privy, I reached sleepily for my boots, which were near my feet on the deck of the shelter. When I tried to put the left boot on, something stopped my heel from going in all the way. I quickly took my foot out of the boot, grabbed my head lamp and was shocked to see that most of the raisin fudge-spaghetti mixture was now balled up in the heel of my boot. Dumbfounded, I dumped the stuff out, cleaned the boot as best I could and put it on. Later, still

218

Georgia

before sunrise, I awoke needing to go out again. This time I carefully looked into the heels of my boots with my head lamp before putting my feet in. Thankfully I saw nothing. But then, when I tried to put my foot into my boot, I could not get it in all the way. I could not believe it! This time the mice had put the mixture down into the toe section. I was flabbergasted. I hit the boot against the shelter deck, and the stuff came flying out all over the place. This time I threw it into the fire pit. Why those creatures worked all night doing that was beyond me.

Sunset, Sunrise

I awoke at dawn on a beautiful day. At 30 degrees, the morning temperature was the warmest it had been in a long time, and after I hiked just five miles to the top of Tray Mountain, the thermometer read almost 70 degrees! That was glorious. I hiked down with people who were out for the day, then climbed Rocky Mountain. From there the trail fell away steeply to Unicoi Gap before climbing over Blue Mountain. I stopped to rest at Blue Mountain Shelter. It was another seven and a half miles to Low Gap Shelter, where I was planning to stay for the night. After hiking only a little more than two miles along the ridge, I came to Chattahoochee Gap and sensed that God wanted me to stay there. I camped in total isolation. Chattahoochee Spring, which had the water I needed, was a 175-yard plunge down the ridge. (This, by the way, is the birthplace of the Chattahoochee River, which supplies drinking water for Atlanta and other cities in Georgia. In 500 miles from this spot, the river empties into the Gulf of Mexico.) After gathering two gallons of delicious water from this spring, I climbed back up and got out my tent.

Descending Yellow Mountain in the Standing Indian Wildlife Management Area in North Carolina.

It was silent and still around the gap as the sun slowly began to set on the horizon. I could not believe the awesome, colorful display of the grand sunset that evening. Each minute into the night would send vibrant new waves of colors splashing onto the clouds, which were sitting over the mountains to the west on the horizon. The calm twilight soon followed, and dusk turned into darkness as the stars came out. One by one, and then by the thousands, the stars lit up the eternal skies with fires of their own. God was evident in every tree, leaf and rock on that peaceful ridge, and His presence flowed around and through me all night.

The next morning was also lovely. With the temperature nearing 60 degrees, it almost seemed like spring. As I hiked the ridge near Low Gap, I met Chip and Don, who were hiking for a week on the trail to train for a 100-mile bicycle race. I continued on the steep descent and ascent out of Tesnatee Gap. After going over Cowrock Mountain, I had to decide whether to do three more miles over Levelland Mountain to Neels Gap or camp on the ridge

I cried just about every day on my last week of walking through Georgia. Here I am deep in thought on Rocky Mountain in the Chattahoochee National Forest.

I camped alone on Chattahoochee Gap, yet God's presence was so near during that day and night.
"From the rising of the sun to the going down of the same, the name of the Lord is to be praised."
(Psalm 113:3)

Georgia

As the sun melted into the horizon, the sky filled with fiery waves of brilliant color, and God's peace descended on Chattahoochee Gap.

again. I opted to go on and came into Neels Gap about an hour before sunset. The trail went right by Jeff and Dorothy's Walasi-Yi Center. Normally from March through May, when hundreds of northbounders pass through the gap, a hiker hostel is open.

On a bleak evening in early February, though, I did not know what to expect when I knocked at the home next to the closed store. The door opened, and I was greeted by Jeff and two lovely children named Jenny and Chris. Dorothy was out of town, but Jeff invited me in, fixed me a great salad and a bowl of cereal with a banana. He even did my laundry. Then he arranged for me to stay the night at Goose Creek Cabins down the road. In return for this kindness, I asked God to bless Jeff and his family. Within a half an hour the owner of the cabins, Keith, came to pick me up. He drove me to a peaceful, secluded cabin in the woods, in which I took a long hot shower and put on clean clothes. I was in the lodge making phone calls when Retter, Keith's wife, presented me with a huge plate of food. What a blessing! And after I finished that, she brought me another one. Then we sat in front of a big fireplace and talked for a while before I retired. The cabin was cozy and warm. I slept peacefully. *"God has been so good to me. May His blessings also be with Keith, Retter and their family."*

I woke up late and decided to spend another day at the cabins. In the afternoon Keith and I went to the post office and grocery store. I bought a barbecued chicken, chips and a jar of salsa, returning to the cabin to feast alone. There was such a peace around these cabins that I did not want to leave just yet. Keith asked me if I wanted to stay an extra night. How could I refuse? In the morning we talked for hours in the lodge with Paul, a friend of his. After lunch I helped Keith crush cans before the two of us went to the store for supplies. Many of Keith's and Retter's friends came by in the afternoon. That evening Joel and Gretta, Keith's daughter and son-in-law, had me to their trailer for dinner. Arriving back at the cabin late, I packed, ready at last to head toward Springer Mountain. Joel picked me up at 7:15 a.m. sharp and drove me to the Walasi-Yi Center in Neels Gap. There I got my last mail drop and talked to people in the center. I met hikers there as well, including Gator, Wolf, and The Maniac. Gator had thru-hiked in 1988. Wolf had done the same in 1990 and would do it again in 1991. Maniac, who had also thru-hiked in 1990, was now training for a speed thru-hike, hoping to become the fastest person to have hiked the trail end to end.

Anticipation

Finally, after two wonderful days of rest, I was climbing Blood Mountain through clouds and fog, just 30 miles north of Springer Mountain. At 4,461 feet, Blood Mountain is the highest point on the trail in Georgia. The going was easy, and the next 12 miles to Gooch Gap Shelter were beautiful. The temperature was around 35 degrees, perfect for sleeping,

"It is hard to imagine there are only a few days left."

but the wind picked up tremendously and was gusting to over 30 m.p.h. At times it sounded like a freight train as it roared over the shelter. That night I wrote in my journal.

"I am beginning to have so many different feelings. In my hiking I have tried to slow down, to take in all the precious moments I have experienced on the trail. I have cried just about every day since I have been in Georgia, thinking of God's faithfulness throughout this journey. At times I have had to stop and just sit for a while to pray and write down thoughts that have been rushing into my mind. It is hard to imagine there are only a few days left. I have truly loved being out here and believe this will be my last night alone in this sojourn in the wilderness. Even tonight, with its howling wind and dense fog, cannot be described adequately in words. The 15 miles of hiking I did today felt easy with 60 pounds on my back. I don't know how I got to the shelter before dark because I left Neels Gap late in the morning. I guess I just walked, thought and talked with God most of this day. And now it's hard to imagine — tomorrow I will be on Springer Mountain."

"God, I love the awareness you have given me of your presence. Your Spirit has become sweeter and sweeter to me as the months have gone by. I will surely miss these times."

Higher Ground

My last day's hike of 16 miles awaited me the following morning. I had slept well, even with the wind. I began walking into a brisk westerly breeze across the ridge, with many 3,000-foot peaks ahead and as many gaps to descend. When I arrived at Hawk Mountain Shelter, I had only seven and a half miles left before reaching the Springer Mountain summit. With a flood of emotion filling me, I had to stop on the trail and write. *"I have so many mixed feelings going on inside of me at the same time. I feel happy knowing how good God has been to me. I am glad that I will no longer have to carry 40 to 80 pounds on my back every day. At the same time I feel sad to think that the blessing of walking with God in this way is coming to an end. I will long for the wilderness when my journey is completed. I am also excited and nervous about what might happen next in my life. I do not know where I will work when my journey ends, but my trust in God has grown so that I know He will open a door for me exactly where He wants me to be."*

All these thoughts played havoc with my emotions. I had a lot of tears in my eyes as I came to Three Forks, where streams meet to form Noontootla Creek. The trail followed an abandoned logging road lined with virgin hemlock. It was there, after seven months in the Appalachian wilderness, that I began my final ascent of the journey. When I saw the sign that said 2.7 miles to Springer Mountain, tears welled up in my eyes again, and I had to stop because of the difficulty I was having climbing and crying at the same time. Reflecting on God's faithfulness and love, I was so overcome with emotion that I had to cry out with joy. "Hallelujah!"

As I climbed to the summit, a freezing wind greeted me, but every bone and muscle in my body was filled with excitement. When I came to the clearing that has the sign reading "Springer Mountain," all I could do was fall to my knees and raise my hands. With tears pouring out of my eyes, I sang the wonderful hymn,

"After seven months in the Appalachian wilderness, I began my final ascent of the journey. When I saw the sign that said 2.7 miles to Springer Mountain, tears welled up in my eyes."

"Great Is Thy Faithfulness." For the preciousness of this moment, I was thankful to be alone on the summit that day. I got up slowly and set my camera up against a log to take a few pictures of myself standing next to the sign. Then, after praying and gathering my gear, I headed back down to Springer Mountain Shelter, where I would spend the next two nights – a time that would include a Sabbath. I was glad that it worked out this way.

Guess who was waiting for me when I arrived at the shelter on a side trail. Unbelievably, or so it seemed, it was Rueven. I had not seen him in several months, and there he was, ready to spend the last Sabbath with me on the trail. I will never know how he knew when I would arrive there. Dressed in 10 or more layers of clothing under his hunter suit, he once again looked like a huge orange Pillsbury Dough Boy. I settled into the shelter deep in thought and slowly prepared my dinner. Then I lay in my sleeping bag most of the night, just looking into the dark forest, unable to sleep – so many thoughts and emotions were whirling around in my heart and mind. At last, in the early morning, with the wind still howling, sleep overtook me. Dawn came with beautiful colors painting the horizon. The sun rose into a partly cloudy sky, and the temperature began to climb to the 60s as I walked to the summit and found a number of people camped there. I wrote in the trail register. Then, at different times that day, I took walks to the peak. Rueven joined me on one of them. We talked to many of the folks who were camping and then came down to the shelter for my last dinner on the trail – macaroni and cheese, of course.

"It is hard for me to imagine that this is it and I will be hiking down tomorrow. I have come to love the woods and living in the wilderness. The cold and all else that is involved in survival out here have drawn me closer to God. Even now the wind is gusting to more than 30 m.p.h., and it is a wonderful feeling just being here. What can I say? God has been with me all the way and has kept me safe and strong even when I was faltering. His presence has filled me with wonderful peace."

"In the shelter I prayed, "Lord God, may your Spirit rest upon me and guide me through my next journey in life. Thank you, Heavenly Father, for allowing me to travel with you. My experiences, at times, were indescribable, but your power and glory were always apparent. I must return to the valley. Guide me and grant me a new vision for my life. Let my feet walk your path in holiness and righteousness. Here I am, Lord, your willing servant. In tears I cry to you. I have loved being with you in the wilderness. Please go with me in peace now and fill me with your presence each day of my life."

Journey's End

In the morning I again had to learn patience. Rueven needed to use the outhouse, and I did not realize it would take him over an hour to disrobe and then put on all his layers of clothing again. He was still traveling without a sleeping bag and simply sleeping in his clothes. At one point I thought he must have fallen asleep in the outhouse. I had appreciated Rueven's friendship on

the trail even though I rarely hiked with him. Finally he appeared, and after packing up my gear, I said good-bye and headed up the trail for one last climb of Springer Mountain, praying for Rueven on the way. Alone on top, I went to my knees and bowed my head before the Lord.

The sun was shining in a gorgeous crystal blue sky. It was 60 degrees. I felt at peace. The last white blaze on the Appalachian Trail is painted on a rock next to a bronze plaque with a hiker depicted on it. The plaque reads:

Appalachian Trail
– Georgia to Maine –
A Footpath for Those who Seek Fellowship with the Wilderness

I stood next to this marker for a moment and then, without looking back, headed off to hike the eight-mile blue-blazed trail down to Amicalola Falls State Park, where good friends, Paul and Mary, would meet me. They had semi-retired in the Atlanta area, and in the 10 years I thought about and planned for the hike I always told them that I wanted them to pick me up when it was finished. After hiking four miles down the ridge, I was filled with such overwhelming emotion that I fell to my knees again, with hands and staff raised toward heaven. I do not know how long I remained there kneeling in praise to God, but when I opened my eyes, a young couple was standing over me with strange looks on their faces. It was hard to explain to them why I was kneeling with my hands raised on this trail in the middle of a ridge. So I quickly gave them each a small trail Bible, copies of which I carried, and left them. They were quite bewildered, I am sure.

With three frames of film left in my camera after hiking eight miles down from Springer Mountain to Amicalola Falls State Park, I set up this final shot by a stream.

I made it to the base of Amicalola Falls by mid-afternoon and went into the visitors center, where I was given a congratulatory note from Jean Cashin of the ATC headquarters in Harpers Ferry. It was a lovely Sunday afternoon, and I was in a bit of a daze as I walked around the park, not sure what to do. I asked a couple to take pictures of me – the last three frames on the 137th roll of film I shot on the journey. Within an hour Paul and Mary showed up. It was great to see them again. We walked through the park and then headed for their home in Covington, Georgia, about two hours south. When we got there, I took a long shower and then asked Paul for his razor and a pair of scissors. Clean, fresh and new-looking, I came to the table for the wonderful dinner Mary had cooked, and the three of us talked for a long time.

"Boy! I fell asleep with the light on and pen in hand as I was writing in my journal. It is a beautiful morning in Georgia, and Paul and Mary's house is so peaceful and quiet. The letdown I felt last night is still quite strong today. It is hard to imagine that my journey in the Appalachian wilderness is over. Even as I rode with Paul and Mary back to their house, I could feel the pressures of the world trying to take hold of me."

Day 1 of my journey.

Day 220 of my journey.

"It is hard to imagine that my journey in the Appalachian wilderness is over."

I was blessed to remain with Paul and Mary for more than three weeks before my brother, Gary, came down from Massachusetts to drive me home. Paul and Mary's quiet home as well as their godly lifestyle helped me slowly reenter society. During that time I wrote a letter to send to friends and to the hundreds of people I had met along the trail. I also ran along country roads in Georgia, reminiscing about the wonderful events of the previous seven months. I felt that through this awesome experience I was truly changed. I had wanted with all my heart to walk with God in the wilderness and gain a closer relationship with Him. He blessed me with my heart's desire, filling my life with more faith and peace than I had ever experienced.

My prayer is that each person who reads this book will be touched by God in a special way. May you find the glorious joy and wonderful peace that comes from giving your life to Jesus. Every day in life is a journey in which we can hear and see God more clearly. I know that my next journey is just beginning...

Sunset on Springer Mountain.

As the setting sun initiated my last Sabbath on the journey, I came to the southernmost white blaze on the Appalachian Trail.

Equipment

Kelty "Radial" backpack
Everest "Elite" sleeping bag (30 degrees)
    in summer
Marmot Gore-Tex sleeping bag (-5 degrees) in
    winter Thermarest Ultra-light long
    sleeping pad
Moss Starlet tent
Vasque "Summit" Gore-tex boots
    (for final 1,000 miles)
Ground cloth
Petzyl "Arctic" head lamp
Eucalyptus hiking staff
Swiss army knife – long
Silva compass – never used
Whistle – never used
Thin rope

Lightweight two-gallon water bag
2 quart-size water bottles
Garbage and gallon freezer bags to
    keep things dry
Spoon and fork
2-quart pot and pan cover
Coleman "Peak 1" multi-fuel stove
22-ounce Sigg fuel bottle
2 small lighters
4 stuff sacks to hold food and cooking utensils
Large plastic cup
Small thermometer
Polar Pure iodine crystals
"Deet 100" insect repellent
Small first aid kit
Moleskin for blisters
Blistex
Lightweight towel
Dr. Bronner's soap
Tooth brush and paste
Dental floss
Toilet paper
Appalachian Trail guide books
Thru-hiker's guide
Data guide
Journal and pen
Bible

CLOTHING LIST

2 pairs quick-drying shorts
2 "coolmax" T-shirts
1 bandanna and headband
2 pairs "polypro" sock liners
2 pairs heavyweight wool/polypro hiking socks
Lightweight top and bottom polypro
    long underwear
Heavyweight top and bottom long underwear
    in winter
Fleece jacket
Lightweight gaiters
Gore-tex jacket and pants
Light and heavy wool hats
Gore-tex down jacket in winter

PHOTOGRAPHY EQUIPMENT

Nikon FE
Nikon 35-135 zoom lens F 3.5-4.5
81 A filter
Polarizer filter
Small 15-second timer
Cascade Designs waterproof bag
137 rolls of Fujichrome 50 or Velvia
    slide film

FOOD LIST

Breakfasts
    Granola bars
    Instant oatmeal
    Bagel and peanut butter and jelly
    Pop Tarts
    Chocolate "Health Management Resources"
    drink supplement
        Cereal – occasionally
    Hot chocolate

Lunches
    Bagels or bread
    Peanut butter
    Cheese
    Cream cheese

Snacks
    GORP mix
    Peanut M&Ms
    Beef sticks or beef jerky
    Cookies
    Chocolate instant pudding plus powdered milk
    for milkshakes
    Crystal Light for water

Dinners
    Macaroni and cheese
    Sloppy Joe mix (dehydrated)
    Rice pilaf
    Scalloped potatoes
    Spaghetti
    Milly's soups
    Lipton noodle dinners
    Instant rice
    Other instant soups (a lot in winter)

I dehydrated about 80 pounds of vegetables before I left home and added these to each dinner meal. I took vitamins daily. My spice kit consisted of salt, pepper, Spicy Mrs. Dash and curry powder. I carried Squeeze Parkay to add to each dinner for more calories.

Essential Books

Official Guides and Maps of the AT
Published by the Appalachian Trail Conference

Appalachian Trail Data Book
Published by the Appalachian Trail Conference

The Thru-hikers Handbook
By Dan "Wingfoot" Bruce

Many additional books and journals are available
through the Appalachian Trail Conference mail order
book store.

For More Information

The Appalachian Trail Conference
Washington and Jackson Streets
P.O. Box 807
Harpers Ferry, WV 25425-0807
(304) 535-6331

Appalachian Mountain Club
5 Joy Street
Boston, MA 02108
(617) 523-0636

If you are interested in an autographed copy of this
book or in having Ken Wadness present a 45-minute
multi-media presentation to your school, community
group or religious organization, please write to:

Shalom Images
P.O. Box 3334
Framingham, MA 01705-3334

Matt, the Woodswalker, on the trail in
northern Connecticut.

Sunset at Addis Gap, Chattahoochee National Forest, GA.